THE PRIORITY OF WORSHIP

*Turning Ordinary Christians
Into
Extraordinary Worshipers*

GREG DIXON

WESTBOW
PRESS®
A DIVISION OF THOMAS NELSON
& ZONDERVAN

WestBow Press books may be ordered through booksellers or by contacting:

WestBow Press
A Division of Thomas Nelson & Zondervan
1663 Liberty Drive
Bloomington, IN 47403
www.westbowpress.com
844-714-3454

ISBN: 978-1-6642-3876-3 (sc)
ISBN: 978-1-6642-3875-6 (e)

Library of Congress Control Number: 2021912939

Print information available on the last page.

WestBow Press rev. date: 09/01/2021

"Shout joyfully to the LORD, all the earth. Serve the LORD with gladness; Come before Him with joyful singing. Know that the LORD Himself is God; It is He who has made us, and not we ourselves; We are His people and the sheep of His pasture. Enter His gates with thanksgiving And His courts with praise. Give thanks to Him, bless His name. For the LORD is good; His lovingkindness is everlasting and His faithfulness to all generations."

Psalm 100 (NASB95)

CONTENTS

MANY THANKS

First, I want to thank You, my Abba, my Father, my Yahweh-Y'ireh. You have provided the book title, the inspiration, the motivation, and every word in this book. To You alone be the glory.

Thank you to my first readers for your input, encouragement, and guidance: Tom, Dan M., Dan C., Jimmy, Hugh, Roger, Don, Jane, and Trevor.

Thank you, Roger, for sharing your kind and candid feedback. The book is better for your experience and "extraordinary" help.

Thanks, Trevor, for "bringing the heat" and reminding me that it's all theology.

And to Don, my dear friend. Your encouragement and scholarship have always made me a better husband, father, and follower of Christ.

Thank you, Wendi. The cover and graphics look wonderful. In business and now in my retirement, you always have a way of making me look smarter than I am. You're a real pro. http://www.wendicreative.com

And to my Vicki, there is not a THANK YOU big enough. You are my copy editor, my encourager and exhorter, my ROCK. Were it not for your skill, my sentences would be littered with misplaced commas and dangling participles. And so would my life. Thanks to you, our words will make sense. I love you, Vicki.

FOREWORD

How you worship reveals where your heart really is. Worship is not an add on to the Christian life. Worship is at the very core of what it means to know and love the God who created us, who redeemed us by the death of Jesus for our sins and his glorious resurrection, who indwells us through the Holy Spirit, and who has made us his people.

Worship is the only way you can truly respond to who God is. He is worthy of worship! That is why worship is not an act but a response of the heart to the greatness and grandeur of God, to the holiness of God, to the steadfast love of God, to the lavish grace of God, to the unchanging goodness of God, and to the infinite glory of God.

Worship is essential to spiritual growth and spiritual health. A. W. Tozer said that the weakness of the church today is our loss of wonder. The same can be said of the weakness of many Christians. Worship is to stand in wonder, awe, and astonishment before God. Worship is life transforming.

That is why I am delighted to recommend Greg Dixon's *The Priority of Worship*. I have known Greg for years as his pastor, as accountability partners, as a wise counselor, and as a close friend. He does not write as a theologian. He writes as a layman. He writes from life experience—as one for whom worship has been central in his family life, his church life, and his personal daily life.

If you want to enhance your worship or come back to the heart of worship, you will profit from what follows in these pages. This book is, in essence, a biblical invitation, "Oh come, let us worship and bow down; let us kneel before the Lord, our Maker! For he is our God, and we are the people of his pasture, and the sheep of his hand" (Psalm 95:6–7 ESV).

Don Dunavant

DEDICATION

I'd like to dedicate this book to my dad. His given name was Paul Warren Dixon. His friends called him "Pete." We just called him "Daddy."

You will read about him throughout this book because a lot of him is in me.

Daddy was a simple, God-fearing, hard-working man who put his family first. He was born in 1917, the youngest of nine, on a farm in rural Georgia. As a young man he played a fiddle, which attracted the attention of Mildred Jones. They were married at the courthouse in Reno, Nevada just days before Daddy was shipped out to the Aleutian Islands off Alaska during World War II. My mother came home expecting my older sister, Connie. Daddy was overseas for two years.

After the war, they built a small house from lumber cut and milled on Daddy's home place. Then came three boys: Steve, me, and Bryan, the baby of the family. We had 25 acres with pastures and a creek, rabbits and quail, and plenty of room to grow up as country kids.

Mama was the voice of the family. She was opinionated and no one doubted that Mildred was in charge. She was also sentimental and relational. Steve and Bryan are a lot like Mama. So is Emily, my youngest and her granddaughter.

Daddy was different. He was quiet and kept his thoughts to himself, mostly. Connie and I are more like him as is my older daughter, Katie. He could be hard to please at times. He knew how things were supposed to be and he expected us kids to figure it out for ourselves. Daddy was just and fair, and he loved us all in practical and consistent ways. He made sure we all went to church as a family. He was a good provider. He worked two jobs as a stone cutter, was also a farmer, and raised livestock. We were not rich, but Daddy and Mama saw to it that we had what we needed. All four of us kids have grown up to be successful and raise families of our own. His fiddle and bow sit in a prominent place in my study.

Daddy's in heaven. I still miss him. This book is written in his memory and to God's glory.

PREFACE

This book is simply my take on the topic of worship, based on a biblical worldview. To be specific, it's about the worship of God, Yahweh of the Hebrew and Christian Bibles. That God. And if one guy's viewpoint on worship is something you want to read, then it might help to know who the guy is and, just as important, who he is not.

My degree is in Electronics Technology, and I spent 43 years in the information technology business. I am considered an expert on a few topics like barcoding, supply chain logistics, and computer networking. If my book title was *The Priority of the Local Area Network*, you might be impressed by my knowledge and credentials. But, alas, I retired from all that in 2020 so I could focus my energies on this: expressing my unscholarly understanding of the *Priority of Worship* as a practice in the life of the everyday follower of Christ Jesus. So there. You may not be impressed with my bio; who would want to read about worshiping God from a CTO and Technology Evangelist (as my business card once read)?

Well, *you*, I hope! I am a technology guy, but I'm also a Bible guy. I read it, study it, and I look at how to apply it in everyday life. Application is everything. I like to examine the derivation of the words I read and how the Bible's original languages got turned into modern English. *But words are just ink on paper until they get busy in our everyday walk.* I'm pragmatic. I watch, experiment, diagnose, troubleshoot, apply, and re-apply. Then I do what works. That common-sense approach, I guess, comes from my computer diagnostic training. Pragmatism is a word that's gotten a bad rap in recent years from theologians who believe that understanding the gospel is hard and complicated work. They think if we make it too easy, then the unchosen might slip in through the cracks. Well, I resist that kind of thinking. Worship is pragmatic. You figure out what pleases God and what works for you, and you do that.

I am not a theologian. I have never studied theology any more than any other serious everyday Christian might. The Lord has allowed me to sit under solid biblical preaching for years and be part of some dynamic churches. I've been mentored by godly men and privileged to teach the Bible, lead small groups, and mentor groups of men as well. All this training has cultivated a passion within me to know, love, and worship our great God.

In my 43 years in IT, I got pretty good at explaining difficult technologies to non-technical people. I stood on stages and in classrooms all over the world and made hard things sound easy-to-understand. I also stood up in mission colleges in India and Africa and in front of adult Sunday school classes, Bible studies, and small groups for most of those 43 years as well. I've always said, "If you do anything long enough, you can't help but get good at it." So, I guess, if I'm good at anything, it's making hard things easy-to-understand and practical in a way that you can actually do something with them. I'm a natural tech and a natural pragmatist, and people tell me (well, some do) that I'm pretty good at both.

Let me say this: I hope this book is not one you partially read and put on the shelf with all the other books you've almost read. I hope you will actually read it and practice it and keep it handy when you have some quiet time with God. Even if it's just to look at the cover for some ideas. The cover is designed to give you a visual of the kinds of things you will learn to use in your worship times.

One more thing. I don't know how to write a book. Really. When I do write, it tends to sound more like a conversation. I often speak from the first person and refer to "we," "you," and "us" a lot. I'm doing that right now. I'm also a natural storyteller. So, if I venture off for a minute, just be patient; there is a point to the story awaiting you at the end. Usually. I really believe if we can just have an honest talk about worship, and maybe even practice what we learn, then we both can benefit. So there. We are in this thing together.

So, if you can trust a guy like me (who starts a lot of sentences with "So") to teach you about worshiping the God of the Bible, the creator of the universe, then let's go! We'll dig deep but keep it practical and simple because I'm practical and simple. If you're reading along and it gets boring, or you get bogged down with something, then just skip to the next paragraph, or section, and keep going. This book will have lots of little sections, so you can read all that make sense and save the rest for another day. Some people will like the word studies, and others will get glossy-eyed and want to get a snack. But stick with it, and maybe we can learn about God together.

More specifically, we can learn *how to* worship our God, how to worship Him *more*, and how to worship Him *better*. That's the goal of this book. And, maybe the most important thing we will learn is the *Priority of Worship* because, in my opinion, worshiping God is the most important thing that any Christ-follower can do and must do. *The most important.*

So, let's get on with it.

Greg Dixon

P.S., For my blog and additional resources, please visit the website: http://www.priorityofworship.com

INTRODUCTION
WHAT AND HOW WE WILL LEARN

So, here's how this will work. I hope.

To get things started, chapter 1 will lay some foundational groundwork about worship. What does this word really mean? <u>What is Worship?</u> What isn't worship, and why must it be a priority?

Next, we will uncover the rich background on <u>Why We Worship</u> God (chapter 2). We'll talk about <u>God's Plan for Worship</u> (chapter 3), and how and why He designed it as He did. We'll better understand concepts we find in our worship language today. Things like sacrifice and blood, fire and altars. If the history and detail are too much for you, skip to the next section. Some people just want to know *what* to do, and not why. (But don't miss the stories about my dad.)

In the middle (chapters 4–7), we'll develop building blocks for our everyday practice of worship. These worship components fall into three categories:

(a) proper **attitudes** we must have for worship; (b) **acts** of worship or things we can do as we worship; and (c) **acknowledgements** of God's character from a study of His names. In these chapters, we'll talk about building an "altar" in our daily worship using building blocks that become the "stones" of our personal altar. Because this is a how-to book, these tools will help us visualize worship, then actually worship God. Again, once you see all the acts of worship and names of God, you can skip ahead, if you'd like, and come back to them individually when you need them. (There is a separate table of contents for each of these in the <u>Appendix</u>.) I recommend reading everything, but I don't want you to get bogged down and throw away the book.

<u>Romans Chapter 12 Verse 1</u> will need some special attention. It's one of the great verses of the Bible. (My chapter 8.)

<u>Music and Songs</u> (chapter 9) will play a big role in our worship experience. I try to explain them in a way that will help us appreciate these wonderful gifts in new ways. (This stuff is pretty good, if I do say so myself.)

The Psalms (chapter 10) are poetic and lyrical words of worship given to us by some real worship experts. These songs and scriptures lead and inspire us, and we will learn some new and *very* practical ways to use them in our own worship.

Worship as Warfare (chapter 11) will teach us how to use worship as a weapon in times of temptation, trials, and suffering.

In chapters 12, 13, and 14, I'll explain Whom We Worship, which is not as obvious as it may seem. Next is When to Worship. We will talk about the rhythms of our worship, in church, in quiet times, and in our everyday lives. Then we will amplify How to Worship. Things get practical here as we learn specifically to use the tools and STONES we have developed.

Next, we will address the differences between Religion and Relationship (chapter 15). Worship is doing our part to fulfill and maintain a vital, living, daily relationship with Yahweh, the one true God. This chapter may sting a little.

Lastly, in chapter 16, I have a challenge for you just to help you get started. I call it The Fortnight Challenge. (A fortnight is 14 days.)

In the Appendix, you will find graphics, articles, and lists that may help explain or enhance some content (or maybe just didn't fit in the main part of the book). Also, you will find Citations, Sources and Songs. Here I'll cite my sources and credit those responsible for the song lyrics I include.

I have endeavored to create some consistency in how I present and emphasize certain texts in my book. The *Chicago Manual of Style Online* has been my guide.

Scripture passages are indented and always show a complete reference and Bible version. See the copyright page for details on Bible versions.

If I have translated a word from English to Hebrew or Greek, the translated word will be presented as: *ADONAI.* When I use this word as a proper name or title, I simply capitalize it: Adonai. The only exception is YHWH.

When I insert a translated word (*ADONAI*) into scripture, or make any other change, the reference will include: Author's translation added. I will occasionally underline words or phrases in scripture to indicate my intended emphasis.

Words in the text that deserve emphasis are in italics: you must *want* to do it.

Attitudes, acts, and **acknowledgements** for worship are referred to as "stones" and will be presented as: STONE.

References to chapter titles are underlined: The Psalms in Worship.

I like to repeat myself; I need to hear something several times before it sinks in. So, I may say things a few times, in different ways, in several chapters, in hopes you can learn them as well. Be patient with me. My main intent in writing this book, in the way I do, is to help some of you learn to worship our God regularly and comfortably. More mature worshipers might even find a few tips or tools to enhance your daily worship experience. And some of you might be encouraged to be more consistent and make worship a priority in life.

This is a book primarily for Christians, people who follow the teachings of Jesus Christ in their everyday lives. I am one of those. I understand that different Christians worship in different ways. Your worship style may be influenced by your denomination, your church leadership, or just your own understanding of what worship is. These personal differences are not relevant to the core message of my book. What is relevant is what the Bible says to us about worship. I want to enable all Christians to worship God, worship Him more, and worship Him better. This is my purpose in writing this book.

But, if you are not a Christian, or not sure, then try to keep reading anyway. Maybe you will learn something new, or laugh at something funny, or be reminded of a story of your own. If you find that you want to learn more about following Christ, then talk with someone you know who *is* a follower of Jesus. He or she will help you. If you don't know someone like that, then send me an email. We'll talk.

greg@priorityofworship.com

http://www.priorityofworship.com

1

WHAT IS WORSHIP?

Worship is one of those words. As a word, it has a perfectly understandable definition. But it's a word we have redefined. We have misappropriated it to suit our own needs and alleviate some of our own discomfort with what it actually means. You might ask your church friend, "Did you attend worship today?" or "How was worship this morning?" In these questions, we use the word "worship" to refer to

> *Worship has been misunderstood as something that 'comes upon you,' but it is vital that we understand that it is rooted in a conscious act of the will, to serve and obey the Lord Jesus Christ.*
>
> – GRAHAM KENDRICK

a church service (in the former) and to the quality of the music and message in the church service (in the latter).

My point here is this: simple words can become confusing and take on meanings they were never supposed to convey. Worship is a word we simply must understand if we are to call ourselves Christians. *Christian*, it seems, is one of those words as well. So are *church*, *Bible*, *blessed*, and a bunch of others we could add to the list.

So, is a worship service *not* a place for worship? Sure it is. And when we sing in church, we worship. But our worship leaders aren't worshiping for us. The choir is not our designated worship "team." They simply lead us *in our own worship*. Or, at least, that's supposed to be happening in church. But this usage of the word *worship* can have a limiting effect on what worship really is and what it's supposed to be.

So, what is worship? It's an English word that combines two other English words: *worth* and *ship*. When a word ends with the suffix *ship* it denotes state, condition, character, or quality. It also refers to showing, exhibiting, or embodying a quality or state. This definition and most others I use are from *Merriam-Webster's Collegiate Dictionary*.

A person who exhibits the qualities of a good citizen shows good citizen*ship*. We might attribute certain qualities of a citizen to this person. Think about discipleship, stewardship, membership, and fellowship.

Now, think about "worthship." If there was such a word, then we might use it to ascribe certain qualities or attributes of "worth" to the objects of our worthship. What is their relative worth to me? Are they worthy of my attention, or are they unworthy? So, worthship – or worship – is the act of assigning worth to someone or something. In England, a Brit might refer to a mayor or a magistrate as "Your Worship." I might say of my wife, "I worship the ground she walks on." She would like that. So, worship has a broad array of meanings and understandings.

But in church-world we have, perhaps, redefined it some because the true meaning might just make us a bit uncomfortable. In the church, we worship God. We ascribe certain qualities or attributes to Him. When we worship God, we declare His worth to us. Or more specifically, to *me*. What is God worth to *me*?

So we must, first, ask ourselves: What is God *really* worth to me? Worth is a relative equation. What is my car worth to me? I can think of how much it costs to buy it, insure it, maintain it, and fuel it. I can think of how much it would cost to replace it. All sorts of numbers would come to mind if I was asking about the worth of a car. *My* car. But how do I consider the worth of God? *My* God. Not, just what He's worth, but what He's worth to *me*. Is He worthy of my attention, my devotion, my obedience? Numbers don't come to mind; you can't quantify it. It's a pretty hard question to answer.

Take a minute to consider the things that have worth to you. Make a list of just the top four or five. Maybe your house and property. Your car or truck. Jewelry or watches. There is a real worth attached to these things. Not the dollars involved, but the intrinsic value to you, personally. Now, make a list of the people who have real worth to you. Spouse and kids. Parents and grandchildren. Your closest friends. Ok, now consider whether you worship these things and people.

You are probably a step ahead of me here but slow down a second and consider the question again. Do you really *love* your house? Maybe you do. Maybe your yard as well. You get a warm feeling when you are there. You're proud to show off your home a bit for friends and family. You tend to its needs and keep it in shape. You consider how you might make it better and "homier." So, before you get all theological on me, let me say that it's OK to worship your home some. But it might be a little bit easier to associate worship to people.

I mentioned before how I worship the ground my wife walks on. That seems like a trite saying, but it's probably true for me. I really do worship Vicki Dixon. I think about her and miss her when I'm away. I tell her and show her that I love her. I praise her strengths, and I buy her gifts, all just to show her how I really feel about her. I do the things she likes for me to do. Vicki's love-language is "Acts of Service."[1] So, to show my love, I might unload and reload the dishwasher. This is something I don't particularly like to do, but I do it because she likes it. I also have to practice the proper attitude. If I'm grumpy when I serve her, or if I compliment her without any real sincerity, then I might as well have not done it at all. We have been married more than four decades, so I've had lots of time to find out what she likes and practice these things. So, do I worship Vicki? I guess I do. And I have gotten better at it through the years. Right now, we have one granddaughter, Maren, who is four. When she is with us, there is no doubt that we worship this little person. She is the center of our attention and gets the very best we have to offer. We worship Maren. There's no shame in that.

OK, here's the theology. It's OK, even admirable, to ascribe worth to important people or things. It's OK to work hard at it, because the act of worshiping your spouse is a lot like worshiping God. (We'll come to How to Worship God later; but, for now, we're just considering the fact that it might be hard for some Christians to see the worth of God for themselves.) It might be easy to feel the worth of your spouse or find pride in your home or your pickup truck. But it may be more difficult really to understand the worth of God to you. And we need to consider whether we worship our things or family more than we worship our God. That's where *priority* comes in, and we will tread that ground thoroughly as we work through this question together.

So, you can begin to see why we Christians might try to redefine this word some. Why we might try to soften it and make it more generic, especially if we can't accept that God actually might not be worth all that much to us, after all. It's too big or too scary to contemplate, so we relegate worship to a couple of hours a week when we can all gather and do it together. It's easier to do it as a group, in a darkened room, all facing the same direction.

Maybe worship will seem like *more* to me if we all combine our "Godworth" together. Maybe I won't feel so convicted that my worship is, truthfully, insignificant to me. And, at church, we have worship leaders who can do it with us, for us. Talented, even professional, worshipers, singers, and musicians. "Let *them* worship, and I'll just watch and be entertained. The whole idea of worship makes me uncomfortable anyway. It's hard for me. Some people are good at worship. They raise their hands, kneel, and sing. They really get into it, but I'm not like them. I'm more reserved and not so showy. That's just who I am. There's no shame in that, right?"

OK, I don't know if you relate to any of that rhetoric. You might worship God freely and without difficulty. Or you might have real problems with it. Or maybe you're just somewhere in between (like I am). But trust me when I say this: if you believe in the God of the Bible, if you are a believer in and follower of Jesus Christ, then worship is <u>not an option</u> for you. And when I say worship, I don't mean church attendance; you don't "attend" worship. And I don't mean singing along with the choir, although both of those are good things. They occupy the Sunday morning traditions of millions of Christians around the world. But, worship, *true worship*, must be a key part of your lifestyle as a Christian. It must become a *priority* for every day, not just Sundays. God is not just your God on Sunday, right?

So, what is God really worth to you? Ask yourself this question. Do it right now. What is God worth to me?

If you are struggling with this, don't worry. This is only chapter 1.

2

WHY WE WORSHIP

We live in upstate South Carolina in Anderson, a small town about a half hour from Clemson University. I attend NewSpring Church. We're a big church with our main campus here in Anderson and campuses all over the state, including one in Clemson. Now if you are a college football fan, to any degree, then this example will make sense. The Clemson football program has launched into the national

> *Worship is not an experience. Worship is an act, and this takes discipline. We are to worship "in spirit and in truth." Never mind about the feelings. We are to worship in spite of them.*
>
> – ELISABETH ELLIOT

spotlight in the past few years under the leadership of a guy named Dabo Swinney. As I write these words, Clemson has six consecutive ACC titles and two national titles all under Coach Swinney. Dabo, as he likes to be called, has this unassuming, "country boy" kind of personality that has endeared him to Clemson fans here in the rural south. Dabo is also a very strong Christian; he's unashamed to give God the glory on national TV for everything that happens with his football team. He's unafraid, in this politically correct atmosphere in America, to share his Christian faith with the young men he leads. That's just who he is.

Vicki and I have had the opportunity to attend many games at Death Valley (the Clemson stadium), as well as a couple of the big national games in Tampa and Dallas. Our daughter Katie danced on the Rally Cats, the Clemson Tigers' dance team. We have "tailgated" on campus with other Clemson fanatics and, wherever we go, Clemson fans are a wonderful and rowdy bunch. I'm sure other schools have great fans as well, but I can only speak of "Clempson" fans. (It's pronounced down here with a "p" in the middle. Don't ask.) Orange and purple. (Again, don't ask.) Where we live, Clemson college football is a *big* deal.

As you can imagine, NewSpring's campuses and probably most other churches in Upstate SC are awash in orange attire after a big win on Saturday. If I come to church on a Sunday morning and walk through the atrium to the sanctuary, only the greeters really notice. My friends might say, "Hey Greg," but I'm not a big deal at NewSpring. On the other hand, if Dabo walked through our atrium or most other church atriums on a Sunday morning, he would attract a mob all wanting to shake his hand and call him "Coach." The local TV stations might even have a camera crew on site. Dabo, just by his presence, would disrupt the whole show. He is that beloved by Clemson fans. Now, if he brought with him a young man by the name of Trevor Lawrence (6 feet 6 inches with golden locks), young girls might squeal and swoon. Trevor, Clemson's phenom quarterback, was actually baptized at NewSpring as a college freshman. (That's a hilarious story for another time!)

OK, okay! What's all this about? If you haven't already figured it out, lots of people *worship* Clemson football and Coach Dabo and even young Trevor. *Worship!* I'm not kidding, and I'm just as guilty. Clemson is a HUGE deal around here, probably close to an idol, and we are unashamed to show it. (By now, Trevor is probably a big deal in the NFL.)

But maybe we should be more careful. Clemson worship is not a bad thing. It's fun, and God is not threatened by Trevor's QB skills or his good looks. Still, we should all be aware of what and who we worship. Maybe you have your own team. Maybe you get a little obsessed over something or someone in your life. That's fine. But just ask yourself, "Do I worship God with the same fervor as I do _____? Do I love _____ more than I love God? Does my life demonstrate to others whom I love most? Would someone who knows me say, 'Yeah, I know Greg. He's a big fan of Jesus.' Does my life show that?"

You might be saying to yourself right now, "Yeah, but worship is a private thing that nobody needs to see." Is it? What does your life and lifestyle say about whom or what you worship? What about those closest to you, those who see everything? What if they were asked to evaluate what you value most. What would they say? And what would I say about myself? Do I love the Lord with all my heart and soul and strength? Am I unashamed to show it? Or do I just let that be "private" and unseen by anyone, maybe even God Himself?

"God knows I love him. He knows everything," you might say. So, why do we even go to church? Why would I write a book on the subject? What's the big deal after all? What is God really worth to me? So... why worship?

Blaise Pascal was a French philosopher, mathematician, and theologian from the middle 17th century. He is famously misquoted on his notion of a "God-shaped void" in every person. Here is his actual quote from his work, *Pensees* (Thoughts).[2] (Translated from French to English.)

"What is it then that this desire and this inability proclaim to us, but that there was once in man a true happiness of which there now remain to him only the mark and empty trace? Which he in vain tries to fill from all his surroundings, seeking from things absent the help he does not obtain in things present? But these are all inadequate, because the infinite abyss can only be filled by an infinite and immutable object, that is to say, only by God Himself."

Now, may I paraphrase it like this:

Every person has a craving that was once true happiness, before the Fall, but is now an empty void. We try in vain to fill this emptiness with things that can never satisfy, because it can be filled only with the infinite and unchangeable God Himself.

God made people – us – to worship. It's in our design and DNA. Since the Fall of man, we have tried to fill this emptiness with anything that seems right at the time. For some, religious practice is the way to fill this void. For others, drugs or alcohol are the only medicine that seems to satiate our need or soothe our pain. *We will worship something, or someone.* We will because we just can't help it. We have an inborn vacuum that only the true and living God can fill.

When the Apostle Paul visited Athens, Greece, he spoke about God to religious philosophers in a way they might understand:

"And he is not served by human hands, as if he needed anything, because he himself gives all men life and breath and everything else. From one man he made every nation of men, that they should inhabit the whole earth; and he determined the times set for them and the exact places where they should live. God did this so that men would seek him and perhaps reach out for him and find him, though he is not far from each one of us. 'For in him we live and move and have our being.' As some of your own poets have said, 'We are his offspring.'" (Acts 17:25–28, NIV84)

God created this beautiful world and placed humankind in the midst of its glory that we might see it, be drawn to Him, and desire to seek Him. And if we do, He is not hard to find – not far away.

OK, enough philosophy. I'm not very good at it anyway.

True Worshipers

Go get your Bible. I'll wait. . . . .
OK, now find John 4:23-24.

(It's important for your Bible to be open while we do this next thing. In fact, you might want to look up scripture references just to see them in your own Bible and read them in your version.)

In these words, Jesus is speaking to a woman of Samaria, a nation and people who had redefined the whole concept and tradition of worshiping God.

> "But an hour is coming, and now is, when the true worshipers will worship the Father in spirit and truth; for such people the Father seeks to be His worshipers. God is spirit, and those who worship Him must worship in spirit and truth." (John 4:23–24, NASB95)

There's a lot of theology in these two verses. We'll unpack some of that in a few minutes. But let's just stay with this one word for now: "worship" (or "worshipers"). [3] It appears five times in two short verses.

As you read these words of Jesus in English, keep in mind that He actually spoke to this woman in Aramaic, the everyday language of the people of the Near East in the first century. But this translation to English gets harder still; the New Testament book of John and all the other New Testament books were recorded originally in the Greek language. Greek was the common written and spoken language of the much broader Roman Empire. So, John, the writer, translated the Aramaic word for worship into the Greek word for worship. And it's this Greek word that we translate into English: *PROSKUNEO*. Try to pronounce that. PRO – SKU – NEO. It literally means to show reverence for, to bow down before, to fall prostrate before. It's the word that refers to the act of worshiping God. And Jesus, in his native Aramaic tongue, spoke of worship to this woman by the well in Samaria.

Context is important here, as always when studying any passage of scripture. Go back and read the beginning of John 4. Jesus is traveling from Jerusalem, in the south of Israel, to his home in Galilee in the north. He could have bypassed Samaria, as was the custom of the Jewish people. Why? Samaria was the hated northern remnant of the split nation of Israel after the rule of King Solomon. The Assyrians overran this northern kingdom and repatriated the Jewish people to other parts of their empire. Outsiders were brought into this area, now called Samaria, and produced a new population whom orthodox Jews of Jerusalem and the southern kingdom considered crossbreeds, an unclean people. Jews would travel around this area to avoid having to interface with Samaritans. But Jesus would have none of this! He traveled right through Samaria, bringing His closest disciples with Him. I'm sure they were nervous and curious about this route. But Jesus knew He was sent for the salvation of all peoples, not just for the Jews.

As the disciples went into the village to buy food, Jesus found Himself alone at this well, but had no way to get a drink. So, He asked this Samaritan woman if she would give Him a drink of water. This simple request started a conversation that would lead to the salvation of many Samaritan people in her nearby village. Jesus, uncovering the woman's sinful past, confronted her with it. And, as many of us might do in that situation, she changed the subject. Her new topic was worship.

> "Our fathers worshiped on this mountain, and yet you Jews say that in Jerusalem is the place where one must worship." (John 4:20, NASB95)

It was true that the Samaritans, because of their mixed lineage, worshiped many gods alongside their worship of the One True God of Israel. The Jews worshiped the God of their forefathers, Abraham, Isaac, and Jacob, in the place God specified, the Jerusalem temple. But Jesus knew that both Samaritans and Jews had strayed far from the worship God desired, even required. So, He spoke of a time to come when people would worship the One True God, not at one place or another, but "true worshipers" who would worship God in spirit and in truth.

Later in this conversation, Jesus identified Himself as the Messiah, the Chosen One, anticipated by both Jews and Samaritans. With the coming of the Messiah, a new order of worship would come as well. Because God is Spirit, true worshipers would worship in spirit. And because Jesus Himself is the truth of the gospel to all mankind, true worshipers would worship in truth. This gospel is the "good news" that the old way had passed, and the new Way had come. The new Way regarding righteousness, forgiveness, worship, and so much more.

From this wonderful story of Jesus and the woman at the well, we see several pertinent things for *our* topic of worship. First, worship is important in the grand scheme of the Christian life. Very important. Second, when Jesus referred to "true worshipers," He implied that worshipers (or how they worshiped) could be wrong in some way, incomplete, or even false. And third, we begin to see that the worship God now wanted was different than before. He said the Father was seeking those who would worship Him in this new way, not as part of a religion or religious practice, but in a personal way by communing in spirit and in truth. The two new components yet to be revealed to these "true worshipers" were, specifically, the Spirit and the Truth.[7]

"Jesus said to him, 'I am the way, and the truth, and the life. No one comes to the Father except through me.'" (John 14:6, ESV)

"And I will ask the Father, and he will give you another Helper, to be with you forever, even the Spirit of truth, whom the world cannot receive, because it neither sees him nor knows him. You know him, for he dwells with you and will be in you." (John 14:16–17, ESV)

In essence, what Jesus is telling the Samaritan woman is this:

With the help of the Holy Spirit, we will worship The Father through Jesus.

This concept is a simple, but profound, worship principle to take in! You might want to spend a few minutes and listen to God about it. Ask Him to reveal to you the truth of these scriptures from the Gospel of John.

Ask Him to help you better understand worship, then wait a few minutes and listen. Just listen.

Afterward, if you have some thoughts, write them down.

_____

_____

_____

_____

_____

_____

_____

_____

_____

_____

_____

3

GOD'S PLAN FOR WORSHIP

Old Testament Worship

Worship in the Bible has a language all its own. When you study "worship" in the scripture, you'll hear about sacrifice and lambs and bulls and doves. You'll have to endure bloody scenes that sound like they brought the slaughterhouse right into church. You'll read about priests and the roles they play. You'll learn all about the

> *We are saved to worship God. All that Christ has done in the past and all that He is doing now leads to this one end.*
>
> – A.W. TOZER

tabernacle, then Solomon's Temple, then the Second Temple, then Herod's Temple. (King Herod rebuilt the Second Temple.)

Inside Solomon's Temple there were separate places for men and women to worship. The courtyard held the largest of the five altars where most of the animal sacrifices took place. Inside was a Holy Place, and an even holier place called the Holy of Holies, separated by a thick curtain called "The Veil." Only the High Priest could go behind the veil once a year.

Within the Holy of Holies was the Ark of the Covenant, a big gold-covered box with golden angels on the lid. The ark held the actual stone tablets with the Ten Commandments that Moses brought down from the mountain. The Israelites called this box "The Mercy Seat"; it was said that the presence of God lingered here inside the Holy of Holies. When the high priest entered this special place, the lower priests would tie a rope around his foot just in case he displeased God in some way while he was in there. This way, they could drag out the body.

Inside this holy temple of God were lots of artifacts that all held special meaning. These bowls, lampstands, and tables were made of gold and special wood. The priests had a schedule of specific duties that they carried out in exacting detail.

Every bit of it, every nail and stitch, every measurement and action were specified by God Himself. Animal sacrifice was perhaps the most prominent aspect of temple worship as it went on almost constantly. The altar sat outside the main temple building in the courtyard. A huge fire was built here, and temple priests constantly tended it so that it never burned out. This fire was meant to consume the slaughtered animals brought as an atonement for sins. All of this, the temple regalia, the priests, and the sacrifices were done in the name of worship. God designed it this way, and this was His way for 1400 years.

I've included a few pictures to help you visualize temple sacrifices. Having a picture in your mind will help later.

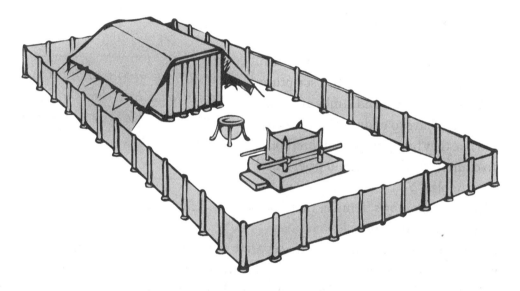

Representation of the tabernacle. Take note of the altar with its
four horns and the laver for ceremonial washing.

Illustration of Solomon's Temple with a close-up of the bronze and stone altar below. Take note especially of the stonework that makes up the altar.

In chapter 2 we saw Jesus talking to a peasant woman by a well in the middle of nowhere. He said things about a whole new way of worship. A way that sounded nothing like what the Jewish people had known for centuries.

If we are ever going to understand the new way of worship that Jesus is ushering in, then we had better understand the one He's ushering out and the conflict this revolution was bound to create. This conflict would ultimately bring Jesus before a criminal trial and on to His execution.

So, let's go from the New Testament back to the Old and see if we can get our hands and minds around Old Testament worship even more.

The very first instance of worship recorded in the Bible was in the story of Cain and Abel, the sons of Adam. They brought an offering, which is the most basic form of worship. No doubt, Adam taught them to do this; and, no doubt, Adam heard it from his Father, God. The first time the word for "worship" occurs in scripture is in Genesis 22:5 when Abraham told his servant to stay back while he and Isaac went forward to "worship."

In the New Testament, we translate the Greek word – *PROSKUNEO* – to the English word WORSHIP. Much of our English language was derived from Greek and Latin, so it's a bit easier for us to pronounce Greek words. The Old Testament was written in the Hebrew language which contains sounds that our English mouths just can't easily form.

(For instance, when you see *CH* in a Hebrew word, make a sound like you are clearing your throat to spit. KKHHH. The Hebrew word we translate *worship* is *SHACHAH*. This word contains one of those sounds. But let's just settle for SHA-KAH, which means to bow down, fall prostrate, or show reverence.)

Abraham was the father or founder of the Hebrew people and the first to really receive personal attention from God (aside from maybe Adam, Eve, and Noah). There is an important story about Abraham found in Genesis 22 that we will deal with later, but here's the gist: to test Abraham's faith, God required that he sacrifice his only son Isaac. That meant Abraham must tie him up, kill him with a knife, and then burn his body on an altar of stones built to the glory of God. So, you can see here that a blood sacrifice on an altar was known long before the time of the tabernacle/temple. *But sacrifice your only son?* I know… how can that bring glory to God? Makes no sense. But this is a small story that will become a much bigger one over time.

God had no intention of letting Abraham kill his little boy. It was all a test that Abraham passed. In the end God provided a substitute ram for the necessary sacrifice, and Isaac grew up to have sons, who had sons, who became the nation of Israel just as God had promised Abraham. (We will come back to this great story later because there is lots to unpack in it about worship, both Old Testament and New.) But for now, let's just pick up a few basics of Old Testament worship that we find in this story.

First, a blood sacrifice would play a major role. We see an altar in this story, a special place or structure where the sacrifice took place. Also, fire. The sacrifice or offering must be consumed completely. Last, the sacrifice must be costly. Valuable. Complete obedience to God is a big part of the process. Giving away something of great value, just to see it burned up on an altar or poured out on the ground, can be very difficult. But sacrifice is the basis of worship, as defined and required by God, in the context of the Old Testament.

Now let's jump forward from Abraham to Isaac to Jacob and his many sons. Due to a famine in their land, they wound up in Egypt where the nation of Israel grew into a million or more people. They lived there, first in freedom, and then in slavery for more than 400 years. Egypt was God's incubator for His chosen people. We all know the story of how God chose Moses to bring His people out of Egypt and into the Promised Land. During the wilderness wanderings, God introduced the tabernacle. Tabernacle is just another word for "tent," a cloth structure over a wooden frame that would serve as a central place for worship. A place for God to "dwell among His people." The tabernacle or temple represented the throne room of God in the world, the place where heaven and earth met. The tabernacle was ornate and specified in detail by God through Moses to the artisans who built it. But it was also temporary, able to be disassembled and transported as the people moved from place to place during the wilderness years.

God appointed a priestly clan from the tribe of Levi to build it, move it, and care for it throughout their travels. You can read all the details in Exodus 25-31 and 35-40. The people of Israel finally made their way to what was called Canaan, the land promised to them by God, where they would establish themselves as a nation. The tabernacle remained the central point of worship for the nation of Israel until King Solomon, the son of David, built a permanent temple in Jerusalem about 440 years after God ordained the first "Tent of Meeting." Solomon's Temple followed the design of the tabernacle and was ornate beyond belief. Here, Israel "worshiped" God who required His people to bring their sacrifices and offer them to Him on the altar within the grounds of the temple. These sacrifices acted as an atonement for their sins. Along with these animal sacrifices, ceremonial washings also cleansed people from unrighteousness. Expensive incense was burned perhaps to represent the prayers of the people going up to God. Also, other valuable commodities were sacrificed at the altar. Wine, olive oil, or wheat might be poured out and "wasted" there to demonstrate the "worth" of God to people. The various offerings involved are described in Numbers 18. You might also read Philippians 2:17 and 2 Timothy 4:6 for some New Testament color.

The priests were careful to follow the prescription for sacrifices laid down by God. But over the years, worship became more of a ritual to be followed than an act of reverence to God, the Creator. *Worship became more religion than relationship.*

Music in Worship

Music always played a big part of temple worship. King David was a musician and wrote many psalms, or songs, to be used in worship. The Psalms remind us of who God is and what He does for us. They put words in our mouths that we might not be able to form for ourselves. They speak to God, but also to us. There are chapters on Music and Psalms later in this book.

Feasts

God also prescribed feasts and festivals throughout the year to commemorate His mighty acts in the lives and history of His people. The Passover was one of these feasts that caused the people to *remember* the great works God did for them in bringing them out of Egypt. The Death Angel "passed over" their houses in Egypt in the final plague that brought freedom from slavery. Remembering what God had done was (and is) a big part of what God wants for His people.

I taught a Jewish congregation in Israel for four nights several years ago during the Feast of Booths in mid-September. This time of celebration in the fall commemorates the wilderness years when the people of Israel lived in huts or tabernacles. Today, Israeli families rig tarps on poles over their carports and driveways to simulate tents or "booths" where they eat, visit, and drink bad wine. Our group of about 25 folks all sat around one long table under a big blue tarpaulin "booth" in the host's driveway. Holy Spirit was evident as I tried to teach biblical leadership principles to these completed Jews. It struck me as I began that I was teaching them *from their own book*. I was humbled as the silver-haired gentleman they called "Rebbe" would quietly explain the Old Testament scriptures. I quickly learned to be still and listen whenever I came to the OT passages.

You might recognize several Jewish feasts or holidays specified in scripture including Yom Kippur, Passover, and Hanukkah. Only the most orthodox Jews still keep all these celebrations today. Like anything, I suppose the repetition of it – as new generations adjust, trim, and redefine the traditions – will make these practices more acceptable and comfortable.

Take a breather and get yourself something to drink. This is a long chapter.

Tithes and Offerings

I grew up on a small farm in rural Georgia. We had a chicken coop, eight to ten white-faced cows, a borrowed bull, a few pigs, and a big garden. This food was way more than our family of six would ever need. For two years, we had two extra boys, foster kids who had lived just up the road. My daddy was a good provider. We were not wealthy by any means, but we never lacked for good food or other things we needed. We lived out in the county in a small house with five rooms and an indoor bathroom. I mention that because my older sister grew up in this same house when the toilet was outdoors. Daddy worked a difficult fulltime job in a granite memorial business in town; he also ran his own granite business from home. Still, he grew and raised enough food to feed us and a lot of the folks who lived in our small community.

In the rural south during the 1960s, race was an everyday fact of life. But Daddy would never, NEVER allow us to disrespect people for the color of their skin. He might express some disrespect for a person for being lazy, foul-mouthed, "good for nothin," or not mowing the grass when he was told.

Every fall, we butchered a hog or two. Daddy would invite a couple of local black men to join in on the hard work. It would start at the crack of dawn and might end by the light of the big fire that boiled the barrel of water that… (well, we might not want to get into what the boiling water was for). A farmer calls that kind of day "from can't see to can't see." At the end of the day, the men would choose the cuts of meat that were to be the pay for their day's work. Invariably, they would choose the modest portions like the pig's feet, head, and entrails (chitterlings). Daddy would then find the choicest cuts – a fine pork butt roast or two and a rack of ribs – and wrap them up for the men as well. Daddy understood that what you give away should cost you something. It should have real value. *The gift was a representation of the worth he placed on the recipient of the gift.* (Remember this thought for later.)

This concept of giving something you value – the best you have – to God permeates Old Testament worship with the tithe. *Tithe* means one tenth or 10 percent.

> "One tenth of the produce of the land, whether grain from the fields or fruit from the trees, belongs to the LORD and must be set apart to him as holy. If you want to buy back the LORD's tenth of the grain or fruit, you must pay its value, plus 20 percent. Count off every tenth animal from your herds and flocks and set them apart for the LORD as holy. You may not pick and choose between good and bad animals, and you may not substitute one for another. But if you do exchange one animal for another, then both the original animal and its substitute will be considered holy and cannot be bought back. These are the commands that the LORD gave through Moses on Mount Sinai for the Israelites." (Leviticus 27:30–34, NLT)

"'Bring the whole tithe into the storehouse, so that there may be food in My house, and test Me now in this,' says the LORD of hosts, 'if I will not open for you the windows of heaven and pour out for you a blessing until it overflows.'" (Malachi 3:10, NASB95)

When it comes to money or produce or whatever a person values, God is really serious about how we view them. I suppose money is the one thing that can most easily get in the way of putting God first. Jesus warned us that we cannot serve both God and money. Knowing man's heart, God imposed pretty strict rules on how people should view their income, produce, and cattle. These things constituted value, and, like today, some people had much, and others had little.

You may be familiar with the Malachi passage (above) about the tithe. For now, try to see it in the context of a Jewish farmer who raised grains or grapes or olives. Maybe he had a few cows and, like my daddy, borrowed a neighbor's bull. Maybe he raised a flock of sheep and a few goats. He had what he needed to survive and sustain his family. If not, he sold or traded what he had in the village market for what he needed. This farmer may have had some money, but his assets were more likely found in a bushel basket or on the hoof. To make sure every person understood and valued God more than these earthly things, He required one tenth of what the farmer valued most. But wait, not just one tenth, but the first tenth. The best tenth. And not almost a tenth, but the whole tenth.

And this whole, best tenth had a descriptive name. It was called the "first fruits" for produce and the "firstborn" for animals and people. So, what do you do with these first fruits? You bring them to the storehouse? Ok, so think about it this way: a million people, maybe a quarter million families, all bringing money, produce, and cattle to the temple in Jerusalem. (Not a real number but representative of the nation of Israel.) Now what do you do with all this stuff? There had to be a warehouse to store it all.

Remember the priestly tribe of Levi? These Levites were dedicated by God to serve in the temple; they had no other job or income. So, some of the wheat, oil, and cattle became food for the Levites (Numbers 18).

"Bring the whole tithe into the storehouse, so that there may be food in My house…" (Mal. 3:10a, NASB95)

- Bring the whole tithe (a full tenth – the first tenth)
- to the temple storehouse
- so there will be food for the priests and servants of the temple.

But the tithe represented more than just feeding the priests. Yeah, a lot more. Go back and read the Leviticus 27 scripture again. See the part about "You may not pick and choose between good and bad animals…?"

When God asked or required a person to give a gift to Him, it had to be the whole tenth. It had to be the first tenth, the best tenth. The tithe was perhaps a way of God's asking a person, "How much am I worth to you?"

> "You may not pick and choose between good and bad animals, and you may
> not substitute one for another." V.33

Of the goats, the spotted ones were cross-bred animals, where the unspotted ones brought a higher price.

Of the cattle, the young bullocks were valued because their meat was tender, and they represented the reproductive capacity of the herd.

Of the sheep, the pure white lamb was the most valued animal in the flock. Many times, the lambs were the pets of the children.

Animal sacrifice was a grisly and terrible sight to see. As a little boy and teenager, I was around the killing and butchering of hogs and cows. Take my word for it; you don't want to experience it for yourself. So, let's see if we can make sense of *why* God would require such a thing as an act of worship.

First of all, animal sacrifice is not unique to the Bible. There has always been the notion that if God (or the gods) are mad at me then I can sacrifice an animal to appease their anger and save my skin. The pagan rituals from the temples of ancient Greece are full of these stories. So, let's be careful not to allow our imaginations to fill in the blanks with pagan practices we have seen in a movie.

The true story goes something like this: God is pure and holy. He created mankind to be holy as well and to live in relationship with Him. But we fell from that lofty realm when sin came into the world, thanks to Adam and Eve. So now we are all sinful by nature, and death (separation) is the only punishment that will satisfy a holy God. His holiness is absolute. He cannot just give us a pass on this requirement because it would deny who He is.

God is holy, but, alas, God is also merciful and just. He wants us to have fellowship with Him, so He allows, even prescribes in the Old Testament, for an animal to be brought forward, killed, and consumed in fire at the temple altar. Death is the ultimate price to pay for our offence. But instead of our shedding our own blood, God lets us shed the blood of an innocent animal as a substitute. And, as we saw in Leviticus, it could not be a sick or malnourished animal, not even a spotted or ugly one. The animal we bring to His altar must be the best one we have; it is, after all, a substitute for our own death. It is a measure of the gratitude we have for God for allowing such a substitute. It weighs the worth that we have for Him!

So, the best animal must be killed, its blood spilled out, sprinkled around, then burned up to ash. Why the fire? A slaughtered animal is just a few steps away from becoming steaks, roasts, and ribs, so to be a sacrifice the whole animal must be destroyed. The only exception was to allow the priests to keep some of the animal from certain special offerings (Numbers 18).

Over the centuries, many priests fell to the temptation of selling the meat for profit; such was the custom of pagan worship. The New Testament is full of references to buying and eating meat sacrificed to idols or false gods. The whole sacrificial system was a constant source of problems for Israel.

My explanation of the sacrificial system here is woefully incomplete and lacking in detail, so it might still be confusing to you. It is to me. But it's important to understand that our merciful God is also just. He cannot be in the presence of sin or sinful people. He provided a substitutionary sacrificial system to make it possible for His people to have an intimate worship relationship with Him. Of course, the temporary system of the Old Testament would lead to the permanent solution for our sins in the New Testament: one substitutionary death, once and for all. But let's not get ahead of ourselves.

As I told you before, my daddy was a giver. He understood the value of tithing to our small Methodist Church. Every Sunday, I would watch him dig out his worn wallet that he kept in his back right-hand pocket. It always had a thick rubber band around it. He would carefully remove the rubber band and open up the section where he kept his cash. In there was the money we all lived on throughout the week – grocery money, school lunch money, gas money. Since Daddy grew up during the Great Depression, he believed in cash. In the back of that wallet were several bills that were neatly folded in half. As the wooden collection plate was solemnly passed along the rows in front of us, he would pull out this folded money and hold it in his closed hand. When the plate passed by, he would drop in his 10 percent and pass the collection plate to me. As a little kid, I would proudly pass the plate on and wonder at how he had obviously prepared for this moment ahead of time. It was just what he did.

My daddy and my mother were tithers, but they also were generous beyond what was expected. The choice pieces of pork for the helpers were just an example. They froze the rest of the pig and a whole cow in neat white butcher-paper packets, labeled with a black grease pencil, then stored in the big chest freezer out in the well house. (The well house was a small building where the well was. Ours also housed the freezer, shelves for canned goods, and Mama's Christmas decorations. It was always unlocked. Like I said earlier, we lived out in the country.)

Our vegetable garden was the realm and domain of my mother. Daddy plowed it into rows behind a big ornery horse named Bill. Then Mama, with all her conscripts (us kids), planted and hoed and weeded and watered that garden all summer long. In the fall, we pulled corn and picked tomatoes and butter beans and okra and squash and cucumbers and cantaloupes and bushel baskets of other good stuff. Mama would "put it up" in quart mason jars or freezer bags. It was all out there in the well house in the back yard.

In the 1960s where I lived, white folks would knock on your front door just to sit a spell, but black folks would come to the back door. That's just the way it was. I remember many late afternoons seeing my mother standing at our back door talking to a black woman. Mama would put on her slippers and a house coat and find a brown paper grocery bag. They would go together out to that well house. I also remember going "uptown" on Saturdays to get a haircut with Daddy in his rusty old blue pickup. The parsonage, the house where our Methodist preacher lived, was on the way into town. Mama would put together an offering of whatever we had an abundance of, at the moment. We rarely made that trip without taking a sack of tomatoes or butter beans or sweet corn that I quietly deposited by the back door of the preacher's house. No one needed to know whose garden they came from.

I warned you that I was a storyteller and, if I did it, there would be a reason for the story. Here it is. I learned about *tithing* from my father, and I learned about an *offering* from my mother. An offering comes from your overflow. You don't usually have overflow unless you *want* to have it, and you *prepare* for it, and you have it *ready* when it's needed. In fact, the Bible says that God will provide just such an overflow so you can have plenty to share with others.

> "Now this I say, he who sows sparingly will also reap sparingly, and he who sows bountifully will also reap bountifully. Each one must do just as he has purposed in his heart, not grudgingly or under compulsion, for God loves a cheerful giver. And God is able to make all grace abound to you, so that always having all sufficiency in everything, you may have an abundance for every good deed;" (2 Corinthians 9:6–8, NASB95)

When the collection plate is passed in church, it's for "tithes and offerings." The tithe is the first tenth, the best tenth, the folded-up and set-aside tenth. The offering is what you give over and above the tithe. *If your tithe comes from your wallet, then your offering comes from your heart.* From your overflow garden that God has blessed you with, that you worked hard for, just so you'll have enough to be generous with those folks you might find standing at your back door someday.

Reading the Word of God

Solomon's Temple was destroyed by the Babylonians, and the Jewish people were taken into captivity. Read the book of Daniel (not now). During this time, the synagogue was developed, a local building or tent where people could gather, read the scriptures, pray, and worship God. Since there was no longer a central temple, the "local temple" was established. The synagogue was still prevalent during the first century AD. Much of Jesus's ministry, healing, and teaching happened in the context of the synagogue. That's where the religious people were.

In fact, Jesus spoke in His hometown synagogue on a Sabbath day, recorded in Luke 4:14-20 (NASB95). Jesus was about 30 years old and no stranger to those in attendance. He was the son of Joseph, the local carpenter, and this synagogue was possibly His family synagogue. He took the scroll and read a short prophecy from the Book of Isaiah, then He sat back down. The congregants were astonished at how He spoke to them. Then He looked up and said, "Today, this scripture has been fulfilled in your hearing." (NASB95). If He had a microphone, He might have just dropped it and walked out.

I love this story, but I share it with you to illustrate the fact that the simple act of reading the scripture publicly was an act of worship under the old covenant. Synagogues in the first century were local places of worship, and their primary acts of worship were prayer and reading out-loud the Word of God. Our worship still reflects these practices today.

Of course, Jews still worship in synagogues since the last temple was destroyed by the Romans in 70 AD. But what was temple "worship" like in the years Jesus walked the streets of Jerusalem?

Temple Worship in the First Century

By Jesus's time, animal sacrifice had diminished some in scope. Instead of bringing a live animal to the temple to be sacrificed by the priests, a Jewish person might simply purchase a dove from a street merchant for a few pennies. Then the dove was given over for sacrifice by a temple priest. Of course, the dove was often returned alive to the same merchant, who sold it again.

> "And Jesus entered the temple and drove out all those who were buying and selling in the temple and overturned the tables of the money changers and the seats of those who were selling doves. And He said to them, 'It is written, My house shall be called a house of prayer; but you are making it a robbers' den.'" (Matthew 21:12–13, NASB95)

Suffice it to say that by the first century AD, temple worship had become corrupt and political. Religious life was dictated by a few men, scholars who decided how religious life played out by those still faithful to it. The two main groups were the Sadducees and the Pharisees. The Pharisees were the experts in the Mosaic Law and determined how it was to be administered and obeyed. They held a strict code of 613 laws which had been extrapolated from the Mosaic Law. These rules gave them power over the religious community and separated them from the illiterate or lower classes of Jewish citizens.[4]

Scribes were like lawyers who drafted legal documents; they were often associated with the Pharisees. Jesus saw them all as the corrupters of the Law and to blame for much of the distortion that had come to the true worship of God. These groups were also threatened by the things Jesus was doing among the people like healing, casting out demons, even forgiving sins. The Pharisees saw Jesus as a serious threat to their control and influence.

In Matthew 23, Jesus exposes the Pharisees as hypocrites.

> Verse 3 - all that they tell you, do and observe, but do not do according to their deeds; for they say things and do not do them.

> Verse 5 - But they do all their deeds to be noticed by men.

> Verse 6 - They love the place of honor at banquets and the chief seats in the synagogues. (NASB95)

Jesus declares eight woes on the scribes and Pharisees, all starting with "But woe to you, scribes and Pharisees, hypocrites." From there, it's pretty ugly stuff. In verse 33 He caps it all off with this: "You serpents, you brood of vipers, how will you escape the sentence of hell?" (NASB95). You may be thinking, "I just might know a Pharisee or two at my church." "Judge not, lest ye be judged." (Matthew 7:1, KJV)

The Sadducees were the more powerful, rival religious faction that wielded control in nearly every aspect of society. They were the Jewish aristocrats of their day, known as much for their wealth and corruption as for their religious devotion. Their primary role was control of the temple, called Herod's Temple, and of the Sanhedrin, the governing body for religious and legal matters of the Jews.[5] The leader of the Sanhedrin was the high priest.

Sadly, the Sadducees had become rich by controlling and corrupting the whole sacrificial system. They could declare an animal brought for sacrifice as "unsuitable" and require that a new animal be purchased from them. Then the unsuitable animal was sold again to the next unsuspecting penitent. They were the mafia of the day. Jesus called them "an evil and adulterous generation." Now, remember Jesus's emotional and angry response to all this corruption? He stormed through the temple courtyard and disrupted the whole corrupt system, denouncing fiercely the current state of worship in Israel. It's recorded in all four gospels. And, remember what He said to the woman at the well in Samaria. He told her of "true worshipers" who would worship in spirit and truth.

God had His people build the tabernacle in the wilderness as a place where His presence dwelt among His people. He wanted them to know that He was close by, but not too close. He "dwelt" behind the veil that separated Him from the rest of the temple. Only the high priest could ever really enter into His presence.[6]

Solomon's temple became a more permanent place for God's Spirit to dwell. It too had a Holy of Holies with a veil. Since it was destroyed and rebuilt twice, it's hard to perceive of a dwelling place for God among His people. Let's keep in mind that the Old Testament was simply the old or original covenant with God, an agreement God made with His people then and there. This covenant included a physical temple where people would come to express their worship and reverence toward God. But Jesus brings in a new covenant. Under this new agreement, God would dwell not in a temple of cloth or stone, not behind a veil, but in a temple of flesh and bone. In us.

What we need to know about worship from the Old Testament:

- Worship was part of God's plan from the very beginning.
- Worship involves a sacrifice, shedding of blood, an altar, and fire.
- Worship involves the sacrifice of things we value.
- Worship involves a central place where people can worship together.
- Worship can also be done away from the central place.
- Worship involves music and singing.
- Worship involves giving tithes and offerings.
- Worship involves prayer and reading God's Word out loud.
- Worship involves remembering and celebrating the past deeds of God.
- Worship involves spiritual cleansing and atonement for sin.
- Worship is a serious matter to God.
- Worship is a requirement for His followers.
- Worship brings glory to God alone.

Every one of these statements about Old Testament worship is still part of 21st-century New Testament worship! The rest of this book explains how. To understand something new, we benefit from looking at how we got here and what we can learn from the past. Today, we live as New Testament Christians under a new covenant made possible by the life and blood and death and resurrection of Jesus the Christ. With a better understanding of the practices of worship in the Old Testament, perhaps now we might see some New Testament scriptures in a bright new light.

In each of these New Testament scriptures below, <u>underline</u> or highlight the words that relate to Old Testament worship. This exercise will help you learn to spot the worship language of the Bible.

Matthew 27:50–51 (NASB95)
"And Jesus cried out again with a loud voice and yielded up His spirit. And behold, the <u>veil of the temple</u> was torn in two from top to bottom; and the earth shook, and the rocks were split."

1 Corinthians 3:16–17 (NASB95)
"Do you not know that you are a temple of God and that the Spirit of God dwells in you? If any man destroys the temple of God, God will destroy him, for the temple of God is holy, and that is what you are."

Romans 12:1 (NASB95)
"Therefore, I urge you, brethren, by the mercies of God, to present your bodies a living and holy sacrifice, acceptable to God, which is your spiritual service of worship."

Ephesians 1:7–8 (NASB95)
"In Him we have redemption through His blood, the forgiveness of our trespasses, according to the riches of His grace which He lavished on us."

Colossians 1:19–20 (NASB95)
"For it was the Father's good pleasure for all the fullness to dwell in Him, and through Him to reconcile all things to Himself, having made peace through the blood of His cross; through Him, I say, whether things on earth or things in heaven."

Colossians 3:15–16 (NASB95)
"Let the peace of Christ rule in your hearts, to which indeed you were called in one body; and be thankful. Let the word of Christ richly dwell within you,

with all wisdom teaching and admonishing one another with psalms and hymns and spiritual songs, singing with thankfulness in your hearts to God."

Revelation 5:8–9 (NASB95)
"When He had taken the book, the four living creatures and the twenty-four elders fell down before the Lamb, each one holding a harp and golden bowls full of incense, which are the prayers of the saints. And they sang a new song, saying, Worthy are You to take the book and to break its seals; for You were slain and purchased for God with Your blood men from every tribe and tongue and people and nation."

Hebrews 1:1–3 (NASB95)
"God, after He spoke long ago to the fathers in the prophets in many portions and in many ways, in these last days has spoken to us in His Son, whom He appointed heir of all things, through whom also He made the world.

"And He is the radiance of His glory and the exact representation of His nature, and upholds all things by the word of His power. When He had made purification of sins, He sat down at the right hand of the Majesty on high…"

If you're feeling inspired, you might do the same thing with the whole book of Hebrews. With the Old Testament insights you now have, I promise you'll read Hebrews with a new understanding and appreciation for what Jesus did for you.

Just to bring things full circle, let me say (though I trust it should be obvious by now): God requires our worship. God is worthy of our worship. And God has made it abundantly clear what is expected for our worship to be acceptable and satisfying. When we truly worship Him, it pleases The Father, and we are blessed.

With the help of the Holy Spirit, we will worship The Father through Jesus.

4

ATTITUDES FOR WORSHIP

I have a confession. I'm a complete Anglophile; I love all things British. According to my DNA profile, my ancestors were from the north of England and Scotland. I like to read historical fiction by Bernard Cornwell (Brit) and watch documentaries on castles, monarchs, and the British Navy. I've had the opportunity to visit England a few times and spent time in London, Bristol, Portsmouth, Hull, and the

> *The root of all virtue and grace, of all faith and acceptable worship, is that we know that we have nothing but what we receive and bow in deepest humility to wait upon God for it.*
>
> – ANDREW MURRAY

beautiful Cotswold countryside that England is so famous for. I visited Windsor Castle and Shakespeare's home and Oxford University. I just can't get enough of the royal family and all the protocol that has been passed down through a thousand years of kings and queens.

When I think about worshiping God, a lot of what I've learned about royalty comes to mind. For instance, you don't just barge into the queen's parlor and demand an audience. And you can't treat the king with too much familiarity. You refer to him as "Your Majesty" or "Your Royal Highness." You do a lot of bowing, kneeling, or curtseying before the queen. You must show respect, deference, and humility. You would never address the queen with, "S'up, Liz?"

Now, think about worship and whom you are worshiping. God is not a king; He is THE King of Kings. He is your Lord and Master and Creator and Owner. Yes, worship is intimate and close and personal. You can call Him Abba and Father. But, be careful here. Don't treat God with too much familiarity. Don't call Him "Lord" without recognizing what that title says about Him and about you.

God is not the "Man upstairs" or the "Big Kahuna;" nor is He your BFF or best bud that you can just rap with when you get blue. I'm sure you've heard it said, "God is not a vending machine." We show up, a bit desperate, with our roll-of-quarters prayer list, and we start dropping in coins and telling God what we want. Let me assume we all understand this fact: there *is* a place in our relationship with Him for our extensive prayer list. But we are here to worship the King of Kings. How we approach His throne room is very important.

Maybe we could consider this approach: an attitude check. Ask yourself, "What is my attitude right now about God, about worship, about life?" If you are struggling with some poor attitude, maybe bitterness, or anger, or unforgiveness, then it's a prayer time you need first, not worship. I can't stress enough the importance of having a strong and consistent prayer relationship with God. But that's another treatise altogether. Right now, I want us to make sure our attitude is correct and proper for what we are about to do. When we enter into worship, think of it as having been invited into God's holy throne room. Into His presence.

> "Who may ascend into the hill of the LORD? And who may stand in His holy place? He who has clean hands and a pure heart, who has not lifted up his soul to falsehood and has not sworn deceitfully." (Psalm 24:3–4, NASB95)

These words of David speak of "entering into" the presence of God as he questions the condition of a person who wishes to do so. Who may enter His presence? "He who has clean hands and a pure heart." Not a person who has falsehood or deceit still on their account. Such sins, and any others, would require some clear confession and some honest repentance before God. So, before we can even think about entering into God's presence for worship, we must first reckon with our current sins and come before God with "clean hands and a pure heart."

In the next chapter, we will learn to visualize building an "altar" for our daily worship. We will build this altar with "STONES." These stones represent our **attitudes** for worship, **acts** of worship, and **acknowledgements** of God's character in worship. So, as you see these STONES start to appear in the text, just set them aside for now. We'll learn how to use them in chapter 5. (Take a quick look at the Appendix for a visual of these altar stones.)

Now, let's begin by thinking about our **attitudes** for worship. An attitude is a way of thinking or feeling that is reflected in our behavior. Perhaps our first altar stone should be an attitude of REVERENCE. If I revere you, then I respect you deeply and sincerely; I hold you in high regard. And how would deep respect show itself? What would that look like?

As a boy, I was taught to take off my hat when I came inside. In an older and more basic time, a man wore a hat for protection. It was all that stood between him and the sun, wind, and rain. But when he came inside, he took off his hat out of respect for those inside. If

Daddy saw one of us boys in the house with our hat still on, without a word he just might knock it off and make us pick it up. The shame of then having to pick up my hat still stings. When I take off my hat, it demonstrates an attitude of respect or honor. Without my hat, I no longer have my protection so I'm vulnerable, humbled. I'm still a hat person to this day. I wear a hat when I go outside. But I like to take it off when I come inside, out of respect.

As we enter the presence of God, an attitude of REVERENCE must lead us in. And as we revere God, then our behavior should reflect our REVERENCE. What might that look like? Well, first, you might take off your hat, at least figuratively. You might BOW your head and close your eyes. You might BOW or KNEEL or even lay prostrate. What does your REVERENCE instruct you to do? Remember, each time your worship can be different. Some people like variation, and others like consistency. I believe that your Father wants *you* to worship Him. You, with your own personality. But there are some things that are non-starters, like a poor attitude. For now, just begin with a self-examination of your attitude toward God, your Father. Ask yourself, "What does REVERENCE look like for me, right now?" It might be kneeling or bowing. Or it might just be sitting in your comfortable chair. Maybe it's where you find your quiet time each day. Take off your hat, consider who God is, and ponder what He deserves from you. What He is worth? To you?

Next, we must come to grips with FEAR. You can call this respect or something else if you like. No one wants to believe that we should be afraid of God. But maybe we should have some real fear. Many years ago, I was fishing with a buddy, in his boat on Lake Jocassee, a beautiful mountain lake in South Carolina. A sudden storm came up, and the world turned black. We pulled in our lines and raced to the dock. The rain was pelting us, and the wind was whistling the water into whitecaps. We got our boat out of the water and sat in the truck, soaked, and amazed that we got out in time. Then we saw another boat, skipping across the water trying to get to shore. You could hardly see it out in the rain and cloudy mist. This boat was maybe 100 yards from the dock when a massive bolt of lightning hit the water, not 50 feet in front of his bow. The BOOM! hit us like a shock wave, and the BOLT! made a huge cloud of mist on the water where it hit. A second later the boat emerged from the cloud, seeming to plow through a hole in the water. Almost lightning-struck, the boaters made it out safely, but it was AWE that struck my friend and me.

As I write this, today, I'm standing on that very spot, by that boat dock at Lake Jocassee. I can still see it all and feel the shockwave rumble in my guts. That was more than 40 years ago if memory serves me. For my friend and me, we were out and safe, just in time. But for the guys in the other boat, I can only imagine their FEAR and relief in escaping the storm's fury. It's true: our God is loving and kind and gentle, He is also fierce and furious and dangerous. He is not to be trifled with or disrespected. Just read some of the Old Testament. Also consider

Ananias and Sapphira in the New Testament. Remember them? Sometimes God must assert His authority and demonstrate His unwillingness to tolerate even a little sin. So, should I be afraid of God? Maybe. But we should definitely enter into worship with a healthy respect for the God we serve. Sometimes a little FEAR will bring us to our knees faster and perhaps give us a better understanding of who we are and Whom we are here to measure the worth of.

To worship we must also have FOCUS.

I am easily distracted. I'm a one-thing-at-a-time person. I tend to do one thing, then I move on to the next one thing. I'm a sequential thinker. My wife, Vicki, on the other hand, is a do-six-things-at-a-time person. And the thing is, she is pretty good at all six things. She is a random thinker. But it doesn't matter if you are a Greg or a Vicki-type of person, God deserves all of you. Worship should be FOCUSED.

If your friend is talking to you face-to-face and you hear the little tri-tone sound that says you have a text message, then you have a decision to make. Do you interrupt the conversation and pull out your phone? Or do you ignore the message? I guess common manners are at stake here. Your friend may think it rude if you look at the text. Maybe not. But what if you were talking to your boss's boss. Would you hold up your hand and say, "Please excuse me, but I need to check my text messages?" Absolutely not! It's God you are talking to here. So, what do you do with potential distractions? You leave them out, you turn them off, you eliminate them altogether. And you do this in preparation for your time of worship. To tell your Heavenly Father, "Excuse me, but I really need to take this," is not just rude, but dismissive. "Sorry God, but I've got bigger fish to fry right now." Your regular quiet time might tolerate a little distraction, but your worship time should not.

In preparation for your worship, you might turn off your phone. Not just mute it but turn it off. I know your phone might be very important to you; I get that. But remember that SACRIFICE is an important stone in the worship altar. SACRIFICE your connection to the rest of the world, just for these few minutes. Turn it off.

Also turn off the TV. If that's not possible (the kids are watching it) then find a quiet place where the TV is not a distraction. SILENCE is another important stone. And speaking of the kids, they are one of life's biggest distractions. Wait for them to be asleep, or at school, or out of the house. Maybe you are pre-kids or post-kids like Vicki and me. If so, then sacrificing all your distractions will be much easier. Take full advantage of this time in your life. Worship will be a lot easier to prepare for. But prepare we must.

Try to think of some things you might need to sacrifice to worship the Father effectively. Write them down:

GREG DIXON

For 43 years, I drove nearly every weekday to a job. Now, I'm retired. But during those work years, I tried to use my daily drive time in the morning to pray and even worship. I have to say that I got pretty good at it. Life was busy and stressful, and those 30 minutes or so could be a good preparation for my workday. If this is your commuting situation, I recommend worship to you as well. I also like to listen to audio books and secular podcasts. Many times, I'd just flip on the book, right where I'd left off the afternoon before, and get back into the story. But then Holy Spirit would nudge me and say, "Hey, remember Me?"

I had to learn some disciplines for drive-time worship. I learned to SACRIFICE my desires and replace them with God's desires. So, is your drive time a great place to worship? No, it is not. But it can work as an additional time of worship. It can be a good time for worship MUSIC. I love to put on a worship playlist from my phone and SING out loud to God. I can make a joyful noise that no one else can hear. No one but my Father, and He loves to hear me sing. I can worship God in the car, pretty good. But, in reality, I'm not all there in His presence, am I? I must still pay attention to traffic, and red lights, and my speed. I must still drive the car. My safety and the safety of others is not something God would ever expect me to SACRIFICE. So, is drive time a good opportunity for me to worship God? Yes, maybe. But is it the best I have to offer the King of Kings? No, it's not. Worship should be FOCUSED, simply out of respect and REVERENCE for Whom we are worshiping, and you can never be fully focused while you are driving a car.

REVERENCE. That's where we start, and it takes some preparation to get there. We find our quiet place where we can be alone. Potential distractions are set aside, and we bring some FOCUS to our minds and bodies. "What am I here for? I'm here to be in the presence of the King of all Kings."

HUMILITY. This is a correct assessment of who I am, a correct assessment of who God is, and then understanding the difference. Compared to God, just exactly who do I think I am?

Am I somebody? Something special? Nope. I am a subject of the King. I am a servant of the Lord. I don't have an inside track on the will of God. Compared to others, I'm nothing, nobody. I come before the Lord of Heaven with clean, but empty hands. I come before a holy, perfect God, with a purified but naturally deceitful heart. My best efforts are like dirty rags.

Now, balance HUMILITY with DELIGHT.

Am I somebody? Something special? You bet I am! I'm a child of the King, an heir to the throne, coheirs with Jesus who is sitting at God's right hand, ever speaking to God on my behalf. I am a temple of God. Holy Spirit lives inside me. I am ransomed by the blood of Jesus and set free from the penalty of my sins. I am forgiven, justified, redeemed, sealed, and ever being sanctified. I am a new creation. I have become His righteousness. I am chosen, holy, and blameless. I am a part of His body on earth and yet a citizen of heaven. I am truly blessed, raised up, and seated with Him. Nothing can separate me from His love. I can come before His throne with BOLDNESS and CONFIDENCE. Turns out, I am somebody to God after all![8]

If there is one word that can sum up HUMILITY, DELIGHT, BOLDNESS and CONFIDENCE, it has to be the word HOPE.

> HOPE is not a wish or a want. "I hope I get a new bike for Christmas."
> HOPE is not self-assurance. "I hope I get this right. I've got this."
> HOPE is God-assurance that good things will come. He's got this!
> HOPE is the confident expectation of what God has promised.
> > Holding On to Promises Eternal
> HOPE is based on God's ability and His faithfulness.
> HOPE is in God alone.
> HOPE is an attitude, a way of thinking or feeling, reflected in our behavior.
> HOPE is a choice we make.
> HOPE is the cure for fear.
> HOPE is contagious.
> HOPE perseveres.

> "Blessed be the God and Father of our Lord Jesus Christ! According to his great mercy, he has caused us to be born again to a living hope through the resurrection of Jesus Christ from the dead," (1 Peter 1:3, ESV)

> "I say to myself, 'The LORD is my portion; therefore, I will wait for him.' The LORD is good to those whose hope is in him, to the one who seeks him; it is good to wait quietly for the salvation of the LORD." (Lamentations 3:24-26, NIV84)

And all this I owe to Jesus, God's Son, and my friend.

How can I be both HUMBLE and DELIGHTED? What does a living HOPE look like? Jesus has given us the perfect pattern to follow, the right attitude to have regarding our position before the Father. Here it is.

> "Do nothing from selfishness or empty conceit, but with humility of mind regard one another as more important than yourselves; do not merely look out for your own personal interests, but also for the interests of others. Have

this attitude in yourselves which was also in Christ Jesus, who, although He existed in the form of God, did not regard equality with God a thing to be grasped, but emptied Himself, taking the form of a bond-servant, and being made in the likeness of men. Being found in appearance as a man, He humbled Himself by becoming obedient to the point of death, even death on a cross. For this reason also, God highly exalted Him, and bestowed on Him the name which is above every name, so that at the name of Jesus EVERY KNEE WILL BOW, of those who are in heaven and on earth and under the earth, and that every tongue will confess that Jesus Christ is Lord, to the glory of God the Father." (Philippians 2:3–11, NASB95)

If you have been following my understanding of how royalty works in the monarchy of the United Kingdom, then maybe you have a visual of the King or Queen of England, sitting on their thrones, with their entourage all around them. Maybe you've seen a painting or TV show with King Henry VIII, all regal and fat, and beside him is one of his six wives, the beautiful and obviously current Queen of England. Everyone is bowing, with their eyes averted, with all the deference and humility they can muster. The room is big and ornate, and the throne itself is elevated above the level of the royal subjects.

Have you created a picture of our God on His throne? Do you see His throne room? I know God is not a person with a body and a face, but we are visual creatures who need a picture in our minds to work with. John created just such a vision for us in the Book of Revelation. Isaiah also saw Him "sitting on a throne, lofty and exalted, with the train of His robe filling the temple," (Isaiah 6:1, NASB95).

Is God on His throne in your mind and imagination?

OK, now to our left, and placed on His right, is another throne. Seated on this throne is Jesus. King Jesus, the Prince of Peace, the Lamb of God. His name is honored above all other names. He is our advocate before the Father. It is only because of Him that I can even dare to enter into the presence of the holiest King of Kings.

As I BOW in FEAR before Him, full of HOPE, completely FOCUSED, HUMBLED, but absolutely DELIGHTED to be here, Jesus touches the King's right hand, and says, "Abba, she is one of mine." "He's my friend."

And God is pleased.

My hope is built on nothing less
Than Jesus' blood and righteousness
I dare not trust the sweetest frame
But wholly lean on Jesus' name
On Christ the solid rock I stand
All other ground is sinking sand
All other ground is sinking sand [26]

Who am I, that the lord of all the earth
Would care to know my name
Would care to feel my hurt?
Who am I, that the bright and morning star
Would choose to light the way
For my ever-wandering heart? [27]
    Who am I by Casting Crowns

5

ACTS OF WORSHIP

"'Everything, O king, Araunah gives to the king.' And Araunah said to the king, 'May the LORD your God accept you.' However, the king said to Araunah, 'No, but I will surely buy it from you for a price, <u>for I will not offer burnt offerings to the LORD my God which cost me nothing</u>.' So David bought the threshing floor and the oxen for fifty shekels of silver.

"<u>David built there an altar to the LORD</u> and offered burnt offerings and peace offerings. <u>Thus the LORD was moved</u> by prayer for the land, and the plague was held back from Israel." (2 Samuel 24:23–25, NASB95)

I'm a "how-to" kind of guy. In a bookstore I'm attracted to books that explain how to do something practical. Now that I've said that, I really don't remember the last time I was actually in a real bookstore. As I look over the bookshelf in my study, I see books on how to build a log

> *Worship is an inward feeling and an outward action that reflects the worth of God.*
>
> – JOHN PIPER

cabin, how to lay tile, and how to travel cheaply. How to love your wife better and how to defeat squirrels. I have how-to books on gardening, masonry, stonework, and leadership. I have a book called, *How to Write and Publish a Book*. And speaking of that, someday I want to write a book entitled *How to Read, Study, Understand, and Apply the Bible*. I have to finish this one first.

The original subtitle of this book was: "A how-to book for Christians who want to enrich and complete their relationship with God." So, you can add this one to the list of "how-to" books on *your* shelf.

I don't think there is a formula for worship. I've seen a few acrostics to guide you.

PRAY – **P**raise – **R**epent – **A**sk – **Y**ield

FAITH – **F**orsaking – **A**ll – **I** – **T**rust – **H**im

WORSHIP

Wait upon the Lord

    Offer our lives as a living sacrifice

        Rest in His presence

            Sing unto Him

                Humble ourselves before Him

                    Intimacy with God

                        Pleasing Him.[9]

I'm okay with using a mnemonic device to help you remember or just get started. I do it myself and have written a few of my own to make something important easy to remember. But I don't want to take any shortcuts with this topic: our worship of God is just too critical to relegate it to a "quick and easy approach to worship." Step 1. 2. 3.

The Altar

In 1821, Lawyer Charles Finney lay aside his law books and took up the Bible to devote himself fulltime to the gospel ministry. He developed new methods for evangelism and is said to be the father of American Revivalism and the leader of the "Second Great Awakening" in the United States. In his memoirs he explained his methods.

He received much criticism from traditional preachers of the day for "illustrating my ideas with the common affairs of men." He borrowed his illustrations from farmers and mechanics and the like. "I tried to use such language as they would understand. I addressed them in the language of the common people."[10] As a preacher, Finney was conversational in his delivery and an avid storyteller. (I really like this guy.)

One of the things he was most noted for was something called "The Anxious Bench." At the end of his sermons, he called people forward who were "anxious" about making a decision for Christ. They could sit on this special pew or chair at the front. He assured them that someone would be able to pray with them and help them with their decision. Of course, today we refer to this as an "altar call."[10] If you ever saw or attended a Billy Graham Crusade, you saw the altar call used with great effect. Reverend Graham passionately called people to "get up out of your seat" and "come to Jesus," as George Beverly Shea sang *Just as*

I Am. Dozens of volunteers waited there to pray and counsel them. The one job I have most enjoyed in my church life is being one of the people who received these anxious souls, to listen to, pray with, and lead them on to Jesus. At NewSpring Church, we call this job the "Care Team." We're there to care for those who have the courage to come to the "altar." We rarely ever have a service without an altar call or opportunity to respond to God in some way.

Of course, there is no actual altar at the front of our church. Many churches have a stage area where the pulpit or podium stands, but still we refer to the front area of the church sanctuary as "the altar." This area is where you come to respond to the gospel message. Untold millions have "walked the aisle" and "come to the altar" to pray, seek counsel, or answer the gospel call. You may be one of these. I was.

I suppose this notion of coming to the altar is based on some of the history we have discussed here. In the courtyard of the temple or the tabernacle stood the altar. Look again at the pictures. It was made of stone and bronze and had four horns, one at each corner. The inside of the tent or temple was off limits to anyone but the priests. The altar was the one place where an everyday person, at least in theory, could come and meet God. People of that time often constructed an altar at their homes so they could worship God there with their prayers and sacrifices. It might have been a stack of stones where they could build a fire and control it well enough to consume a sacrificial offering. Unfortunately, over the years, this altar has become a shrine in many homes, a place to display a crucifix or icons of their faith. But the idea of coming to the altar for your worship is still a good one.

For the purposes of our learning about the practice of worship, I want us to consider the idea of "building" our own stone altar, where we might come to worship. I want us to consider this important idea:

The altar is where God and man meet.[11]

Prior to the tabernacle, an Old Testament altar was simply a stack of rough stones with bigger ones at the bottom. It rose up in a pile with a platform at the top for the fire and burnt offering. It served as a focal point for the worship of YHWH. Consider the difference in killing an animal for food, versus sacrificing it for worship. The only practical difference was the altar.

There is an interesting account in 1 Samuel 7. God had again given Israel a miraculous victory over the dreaded Philistines. The prophet Samuel set up a stone and named it Ebenezer, "The Stone of Help." This stone evoked the fact that YHWH had helped them get this far. When they looked at the Ebenezer stone, it reminded them of God's help.

We might think of "our" altar STONES as simply focal points for our worship. Our altar stones might remind us of God's provision, His healing, His sufficiency, and His peace. How He has gotten us this far.

If we have the right STONES, we might be able to stack them up to represent a place where we might meet with God. And, as with the movable tabernacle, we might be able to take down our altar and restack the stones tomorrow, for a different worship experience, one more suitable for the day at hand.

Building our Altar

Look at the cover of this book, front and back, and consider the stones you see there. One purpose of this book is to introduce you to "stones" that you might use in your private and public worship of God. These STONES represent **attitudes**, **acts**, and **acknowledgements** that will enable, encourage, and enhance your worship experience. A more complete list of these stones will follow. (Again, look the Appendix for these visuals.)

So far, we have laid a few foundational STONES with some definitions that tell us *what* worship is. We have looked at some history and reasoning of *why* worship is important. Now it's time to start with *how*.

Find 1 Peter in your Bible. You will want to read most of the first two chapters to understand the picture of worship we are going to create. It's wonderful stuff.

In 1 Peter 1, Peter talks about our salvation, sanctification, and obedience to Jesus. He speaks of the "sprinkling of the blood of Jesus," and that we were redeemed "with precious blood, as of a lamb unblemished and spotless, the blood of Christ" (NASB95), both clear references to Old Testament sacrifice. I hope you are starting to appreciate the tedious path we took to understand Old Testament worship practices in chapters 2 and 3. (If you skipped it, it's not too late to read it. Dog ear this page, and I'll be here when you get back.)

In chapter 2, verse 4, Peter starts a new thought with talk of living stones.

> "You are coming to Christ, who is the living cornerstone of God's temple. He was rejected by people, but he was chosen by God for great honor. And you are living stones that God is building into his spiritual temple. What's more, you are his holy priests. Through the mediation of Jesus Christ, you offer spiritual sacrifices that please God. As the Scriptures say, 'I am placing a cornerstone in Jerusalem, chosen for great honor, and anyone who trusts in him will never be disgraced.'" (1 Peter 2:4–6, NLT)

Every great municipal building has a cornerstone that establishes the position and purpose of the building. Take a walk down Main Street in your town, and you'll see cornerstones with engravings showing when the building was built, who the mayor and architect were, and so on. Here Peter is establishing, first, that there is a New Testament temple not made by human hands, not Solomon's Temple, nor Herod's, but God's temple. And that JESUS is the living CORNERSTONE of that temple. This temple is no edifice made by the hands of men, but a living temple, with Christ as the supporting and defining CORNERSTONE. Then Peter references two prophetic scriptures:

> "The stone which the builders rejected has become the chief cornerstone." (Psalm 118:22, NASB95)

> "Therefore, thus says the Lord GOD, Behold, I am laying in Zion a stone, a tested stone, a costly cornerstone for the foundation, firmly placed. He who believes in it will not be disturbed. I will make justice the measuring line and righteousness the level…" (Isaiah 28:16–17a, NASB95)

Of course, Jesus was rejected by His own people but, despite His rejection, God had established that Jesus would be the cornerstone, tested, costly, and firmly placed. But this temple would not stand in Zion (Jerusalem). Where is this temple of the Lord now?

> "Do you not know that <u>you are a temple of God</u> and that the Spirit of God dwells in you?" (1 Corinthians 3:16, NASB95)

Our worship will be in spirit and in truth. The Holy Spirit helps our weakness in worship and speaks for us "with groanings too deep for words." The Father knows our hearts, He knows the mind of the Spirit, and Jesus intercedes for us before the Father (Romans 8:26–27, NASB95).

With the help of the Holy Spirit, we will worship The Father through Jesus.

If we are building an altar for our own worship of God, for the temple within us that is ME, then, like a physical temple or altar, a solid foundation is in order. Maybe chapters 1, 2, and 3 of this book will suffice as that foundation. Now, using this analogy of building an altar, I'd like to start handing you some STONES to build with. If there is no real "formula" for worship, which there isn't, then it's left up to us to get a set of plans in our minds and start building. These plans are flexible and adaptable for each day's worship.

No two people are going to worship alike. We are intricate and unique beings, fearfully and wonderfully made by the hand of God. So, the only model for worship I could ever give you is mine. After looking carefully at my personality, my fears, my strong points, and my frailties, I constructed a style of worship that suits me. I worship God in a way that I believe pleases Him and brings me joy. But that's mine, and I don't always get *that* right. I doubt that anyone other than me would find my worship style appealing to them. Some folks would call my worship excessive and showy. Other people would think it to be subdued and weak. That's OK. All I have to do is look at all the things that please God and try them out. Put them in an order I'm comfortable with. Stack them up in a way I can manage and repeat and find joy in them.

That's what I want to do for you: I want to lay out all these building blocks I've discovered for a worship altar, explain how each works, and then connect them together in some fashion you may find practical and doable. Some blocks will be easier for you to take up, and some will be hard. And some may not make sense, at all. But, maybe, just maybe, when we are done, you can build a style and pattern and structure for personal worship that works for you. With some practice, you will learn how to enrich and complete your relationship with God, your Father. And become a daily dynamic worshiper!

> "The LORD's lovingkindnesses indeed never cease, For His compassions never fail. <u>They are new every morning</u>; Great is Your faithfulness." (Lamentations 3:22–23, NASB95)

If Yahweh's lovingkindness and compassion for us is "new every morning", then perhaps our perspectives on Him could also be new every morning. Every day that we enter into worship, our perspective on God should be fresh. If worship becomes routine or redundant, then it is still valid, and God will always welcome our efforts. But for your own sake, as well as for God's own pleasure, try to make worship fresh every time you come to Him. If you struggle for ideas, then watch *National Geographic* channel or the *Travel Channel*. Better yet, get outdoors. See the world's riches and be amazed at God's creative hand at work. Watch your children play and wonder at the intricacy of their bodies and minds and imaginations. All these ideas are good, but the Bible is still your best source for the wonders of Elohim and the nature and character of Yahweh. So, read and study your Bible! (Take a look at page 93 – Elohim.)

Music may be the best source for new inspiration. There are endless praise and worship songs, both traditional and contemporary, that will inspire our worship. We will talk much more about these things later but, for now, keep thinking about how to keep your worship new every morning.

So, let's get started. What follows is a "stack" of altar STONES for building your worship altar. Each stone can be used somewhere in *your* worship of God. Even though some stones are bigger or more vital than others, no one stone alone will ever build an altar. The STONES that follow are all **acts** of worship – things you do. In the previous chapter, we designated other STONES as **attitudes** that are important to start with. Later we will see STONES that are **acknowledgements** of who God is.

We are not going to use these STONES to build a permanent altar for our worship. Instead, we will learn to use them to build a whole new altar each and every time we come to worship. We will choose stones that reflect what's on our hearts today. Right now. Tomorrow I may build my worship differently, using a different selection of stones. Sometimes we will use a few stones; other times we might use lots of stones. In church, my worship will be different than in my personal quiet time. Sometimes we may want to SING, and other times we may just want to be SILENT. Like me, you will likely find stones that will become your go-to worship pattern. Once you understand what the stones are and what they mean, you can use them however best suits you and pleases the Father. You can always look at the cover of this book for a quick reference of some of the stones to use in worship. One more thing: I'm not the sharpest knife in the drawer. If there are ways to worship God that didn't make my list, then get yourself a Sharpie[12] and draw your own new stones on top of the stack. I left a few blank for you. Just remember: do the things that will please God, and you will feel His pleasure.

We will use biblical stones of worship that are tried and established components of a strong altar, with JESUS always as the CORNERSTONE. But we will also build in a way that reflects the tabernacle. Each day, we can reassemble our stones in a way that suits the day, or the situation, or the time frame, or the place we find ourselves.

The key to worship is knowing the things that please God. We are worshiping Him. It's not a show or an act. He is not impressed by how skillfully we worship, but how sincerely and humbly we worship. If you don't like the altar-building metaphor, then think of your altar as baking cakes; you have all the ingredients to bake a different cake each day. Maybe you are painting pictures or writing music. Just take these stones or ingredients or colors or notes and create something that you can use and will please your Father.

And, remember: just like King David, don't offer YHWH, your Elohim, something that costs you nothing. Always consider what God is worth to you, and act accordingly.

> Give thanks to the Lord, our God and King
> His love endures forever
> For He is good, He is above all things
> His love endures forever.
>> Forever by Chris Tomlin [28]

Bless

"Bless the LORD, O my soul, And all that is within me, bless His holy name. Bless the LORD, O my soul, And forget none of His benefits; Who pardons all your iniquities, Who heals all your diseases;

> *God is most glorified in us when we are most satisfied in Him.*
>
> –JOHN PIPER

Who redeems your life from the pit; Who crowns you with lovingkindness and compassion; Who satisfies your years with good things, So that your youth is renewed like the eagle." (Psalm 103:1–5, NASB95)

BLESS is a Christian word. "May the Lord bless you and keep you."

BLESS is a southern word. "Well, bless her heart."

BLESS means "to confer or invoke divine favor upon."

So how can we invoke divine favor on the perfectly divine nature of God?

BLESS can also mean to convey or give someone a gift that is valuable to the giver. "My father blessed me with a new car."

The Hebrew word here that is translated "bless" is *BARAK*. It is most often translated as bless or blessed and conveys kneeling and saluting. But this word really has only one meaning and that's "to bless." Here in Psalm 103, one of the great worship songs of all time, King David is leading us in worshiping our great God by instructing our souls three times to "bless Yahweh." There are 22 occurrences of this phrase in the Old Testament, and all but five are in the Psalms. It's not just another word for praise, but it is often used in the same sentence as praise. Psalm 34 is a good example.

"I will bless the LORD at all times; His praise shall continually be in my mouth. My soul will make its boast in the LORD; The humble will hear it and rejoice. O magnify the LORD with me, and let us exalt His name together." (Psalm 34:1–3, NASB95)

Again, David leads us in worship by saying, "I will *BARAK* (bless) *YAHWEH* (the LORD) at all times." Then David gives up some clues as to what this means to him. He goes on to say that he will continually *TEHILLA* (sing praises), *HILLAL* (boast or praise), *GADAL* (magnify or grow), and *RUM* (exalt) the LORD.

When we hear David leading us to bless, sing praises, boast, magnify, and EXALT the

Lord our God, then we might get the right idea that it's our job to make the most of God that we possibly can. To EXALT Him, to speak of Him in the highest regard possible. We cannot make God bigger, but we *can* make those around us see Him rightly, see Him "magnified and exalted." Our task is to use every word in our limited vocabulary *and* the words of songs and scripture to PROCLAIM to God Himself and others that we are astounded by His greatness, goodness, faithfulness, love, mercy, and grace. And it's not because of what He has done for us, but just because HE IS! Yes, He has extended His grace to me, His love, and His mercy as well. But I will BLESS Him, PRAISE Him, BOAST of Him, MAGNIFY Him, and EXALT Him because of *who He is*, not what He has done. I will bless the Lord continually with my songs of praise, my boasting, my magnifying, and my exaltations. These are ways for me to bless God with the things I have to offer Him; but, now that I think of it, I only have a couple of things to offer God. I have my obedience and my worship, and He wants both in abundance.

"Bless the Lord, oh my Soul, and all that is within me. Bless His holy name."
(NASB95)

Confess and Repent

I want to pull out these actions and allow them to be separate stones. Or maybe one stone with CONFESS on one side and REPENT on the other. They are separate things but should rarely happen apart from one another.

The word we translate "confess" means "to say the same." Holy Spirit might convict me of a sin, and my confession comes when I agree with Him and call it what it is. When we (Holy Spirit and me) are in agreement, then I can express what I will do, or have been doing, to "repent." This word means to "turn around and go in another direction."

In worship, you might just say, "Lord, I confess that my _____ is wrong. It is sin. I will _____ to correct this, so I will not do this again. I want to please you."

If you want, you might ask God to forgive this sin. "Lord, please forgive this sin." But keep this in mind: if you are born again, if you are a believing follower of Christ, then *this* sin and *every sin* you have ever committed, and every sin you will ever commit, *has been* forgiven by God, our Father. *Past tense.* Jesus made this forgiveness possible by His blood and death on the cross. His blood sacrifice was the atonement for your sins and mine. Once and for all.

I have come to the place in my life where I don't ask God to forgive a sin. If I do, I perceive I have put Jesus *back* on the cross. By asking for forgiveness, I am asking Him to pay again the terrible price He has already paid. Instead, in my mind during my worship, I picture the cross empty. Just two cross members and no Jesus hanging there. I know other well-meaning Christians might see a crucifix, a cross with Jesus still hanging there. But to me, this denies the resurrection and ascension and the fact that Jesus now sits at the right hand of the Father making intercession for us true believers (Romans 8:34). *My cross is empty*; that means a lot to me, as I consider my sins, in preparation for worship. I know many Christians are taught to ask God to forgive their sins as they confess them. I'm not suggesting that this is un-doctrinal in any way. But I see this differently now, so my practice reflects this belief.

Dr. Charles Stanley exhorts us "to keep a short account of our sins." To keep them current so we don't let a sin fester in an unconfessed, unrepented state. Don't wait for your quiet time or your worship time to drag out your sin-list and present it to God.

When you come before the Father to worship, be reminded of this verse:

> "Who may ascend into the hill of the LORD? And who may stand in His holy place? He who has clean hands and a pure heart, Who has not lifted up his soul to falsehood And has not sworn deceitfully." (Psalm 24:3–4, NASB95)

Before you begin to worship the Father, be sure that your sin account is up to date. As you stop to consider your sin, you may find, as I often do, that there is some sin you have not completely dealt with. I simply confess it (name it and call it sin) and express my repentance (what I'm going to do about it).

Here's something that I have used over the years that may help you.

> **C**onfess your sins. (Be specific).
> **H**onest **R**epentance (not "I hope" but "I will").
> **I**nvite Holy Spirit to be in charge.
> **S**ubmit to His discipline.
> **T**rust His leadership.
> **C H R I S T**

My forgiveness is already in place. Now, I can enter into His presence with "clean hands and a pure heart." If you are going to use the CONFESS AND REPENT stones in your altar, then they should probably come up early in your worship.

> "If we confess our sins, He is faithful and just and will forgive us our sins and purify us from all unrighteousness." (1 John 1:9, NASB95)

> "Repent, then, and turn to God, so that your sins may be wiped out, that times of refreshing may come from the Lord." (Acts 3:19, NASB95)

Delight

"Delight yourself in the Lord; And He will give you the desires of your heart." (Psalm 37:4, NASB95)

I came across a good book of essays by Ross Gay called, *The Book of Delight*.[13] He wrote an essay for each day of a year about what he found in that day that brought him delight. Here are a few of his thoughts, mixed in with a few of my own:

> *We are perishing for lack of wonder, not for lack of wonders.*
>
> – G.K. Chesterton

- Delight won't just come to you. You have to go looking for it.
- Delight is something to be shared.
- It's a good feeling – but hard to put your finger on.
- You'll know it when you feel it.
- Delight is butterflies flitting around and landing on joy.
- What causes you to gasp with delight?
- We might think somehow that delight is the domain of children. Not so.

Vicki and I have taken RV trips to South Dakota, Montana, Wyoming, and Utah. We were amazed at what we saw there. The startlingly brilliant rainbow colors of the steaming pools at Yellowstone. The monochrome mist hanging over the snowclad granite of Mount Rushmore. A pair of bald eagles preening in their nest atop a hundred-foot lodge pole pine on the south bank of the Snake River. The vast red and tan canyons that cover southern Utah.

You don't have to go to Big Sky Country to see the beauty in nature. "Look, a whole rainbow!!" "Did you see that amazing sunset?" "Look at all those stars!" Did you ever stop and think, "Wow, God did that?"

My new favorite worship song is written by Hillsong. It's called *So Will I*. Here's the first part of it.

God of creation
There at the start
Before the beginning of time
With no point of reference
You spoke to the dark
And fleshed out the wonder of light

In the vapor of Your breath the planets form
If the stars were made to worship, so will I.[29]
    by Joel Houston / Benjamin William Hastings / Ben Tan

It's not hard to find DELIGHT in what God has made for us, but you have to get up and go find it. See it for yourself! Just stand and gasp at it with someone you love. When you do, then remember that moment, that feeling of awe and surprise and joy. Say to yourself and whoever is nearby, "Wow! God did that!"

Like the essay author did, write it down. Then, take a picture. Not a selfie, but a good landscape picture of what God did. Take note of your sheer delight and what it was that caused it. These photos and descriptions are good material for a worship journal. Print out the pictures and tape them to the pages in the journal, with your thoughts and feelings, if you can find words to express them.

Below, write down some of your heart's desires. Then, bring your DELIGHT and your desires with you to worship. [Also see Rejoice]

_____

_____

_____

_____

_____

_____

_____

_____

Fasting and Prayer

FASTING is probably exactly what you think it is. Or maybe not. You don't eat food for some pre-agreed-upon time. The agreement is between you and God. Fasting plays a role in nearly every religion. The Bible refers to fasting many times, but I can't find any real commands for us to fast. God never gives us any rules or guidance on how or how often we might fast. Fasting is often combined with prayer – PRAYER and FASTING – and, as you might think, it is much misunderstood and misused. Fasting can become just another religious practice, or it can serve to remind you of who you are and Whose you are.

As part of your worship, you might set aside a period of time, maybe 24 hours, when you will not eat. You'll get hungry, but whenever you feel the pangs, just PRAY. Say to your Father, "Lord, this is for You." Look at fasting as more of a SACRIFICE to God. You give up something precious, just to honor God.

Jesus had some really good advice for us:

> "Whenever you fast, do not put on a gloomy face as the hypocrites do, for they neglect their appearance so that they will be noticed by men when they are fasting. Truly I say to you, they have their reward in full. But you, when you fast, anoint your head and wash your face so that your fasting will not be noticed by men, but by your Father who is in secret; and your Father who sees what is done in secret will reward you." (Matthew 6:16–18, NASB95)

Fasting is just between you and God. No one else needs to know about it, with the possible exception of the people you might be eating with.

Here are some tips:[14]

- Don't overdo it. Jesus fasted for 40 days, but you're not Jesus.
- Don't cheat on a total food fast. Stay away from food altogether.
- Drink plenty of water.
- Be careful if you are diabetic or have other medical concerns.
- If you start to feel really weak or sick, then eat something. This is worship, not punishment.
- Put on your "*Soul Pants.*"

> "As the deer pants for the water brooks, So my <u>soul pants</u> for You, O God.
> My soul <u>thirsts</u> for God, for the living God; When shall I come and appear before God?" (Psalm 42:1–2, NASB95)

During your FAST, seek God more diligently than usual. Listen to Him. When you are FOCUSED on God, you will hear His voice much clearer. Choose your fasting times carefully. Make sure you can use it to stay focused on God. If you have exams or work travel or some other difficult situation, then maybe that time is not the best time for a FAST. Plan it and when the time comes, give your whole self to God.

> "Therefore, I urge you, brethren, by the mercies of God, to present your bodies a living and holy sacrifice, acceptable to God, which is your spiritual service of worship." (Romans 12:1, NASB95)

Fasting will remind you of your spiritual needs. So, ask yourself, "Why am I fasting?" (Note: I am addressing fasting only in the context of worship.) There are other times and other spiritual reasons to fast. But fasting can be a vital part of your worship of the Father. It will teach you to extend yourself, to go further with God than you might have otherwise. A good time to pull out the FASTING stone is if you are stuck spiritually or stale or just need a reboot.

> "I have set the Lord continually before me; Because He is at my right hand, I will not be shaken. Therefore, my heart is glad and my glory rejoices; My flesh also will dwell securely." (Psalm 16:8–9, NASB95)

Glorify

We are starting to see some of our worship stones show up in other discussions. When we learned about PRAISING or BLESSING God, we were, in effect, GLORIFYING God. To GLORIFY is to increase in value, importance,

or quality. Glory is something you win or achieve through notable effort which God has already done. He has won and earned the glory that He has and deserves. He made the world, and He allows us to live in it. "To God be the glory, great things He has done." To speak of His glory is to encompass all His grandeur, beauty, majesty, and awe into one package that we can refer to with one single word: GLORY.

Some people seek glory. ("Hey! Look at what I did.") Others shun it. ("Awe, that was nuthin.") But for God, glory is what describes His presence. In the first temple, it was said you could actually see or perceive it. They called it the "Shekinah Glory." The word "shekinah" only appears in Rabbinic literature of the times. To Solomon and the people of Israel, however, it was a real thing. They saw it.

> "Now when Solomon had finished praying, fire came down from heaven and consumed the burnt offering and the sacrifices, and the glory of the LORD filled the house. The priests could not enter into the house of the LORD because the glory of the LORD filled the LORD's house. All the sons of Israel, seeing the fire come down and the glory of the LORD upon the house, bowed down on the pavement with their faces to the ground, and they worshiped and gave praise to the LORD, saying, 'Truly He is good, truly His lovingkindness is everlasting.'" (2 Chronicles 7:1–3, NASB95)

The glory of God was a terrifying and awe-inspiring thing. It was His actual presence among His people! Their only possible response was to fall flat on their faces and worship. And what did the people say? "Truly He is good, truly His lovingkindness is everlasting." (Seems kind of uninspiring for having just seen the glory of God.) But humans just can't out-glorify the actual glory of God. There was nothing anyone could say that would do justice to seeing the Shekinah Glory of God. This is true for us as well. What could I possibly say or do to add to the glory of God Almighty? "God, you are big and awesome!" "No, *really* big and *really* awesome!"

Lots of times in my worship, words just fail me. How can I bless a God who is the source of all blessing? How can I praise a God who is beyond any praise of men? What could I possibly do to bring glory to the visible Shekinah Glory of the Creator of the Universe?

Yet, David, a man after God's own heart, leads us to do just that.

> "I will tell of Your name to my brethren; In the midst of the assembly I will praise You. You who fear the Lord (*YHWH*), praise Him; All you descendants of Jacob, <u>glorify Him,</u> And stand in awe of Him, all you descendants of Israel." (Psalm 22:22–23, NASB95 Author's translation added)

> "All nations whom You have made shall come and worship before You, O Lord (*ADONAI*), And they shall <u>glorify Your name</u>. For You are great and do wondrous deeds; You alone are God (*ELOHIM*). Teach me Your way, O Lord (*YHWH*); I will walk in Your truth; Unite my heart to fear Your name. I will give thanks to You, O Lord (*ADONAI*), my God (*ELOHIM*), with all my heart, And will <u>glorify Your name forever.</u>" (Psalm 86:9–12, NASB95 Author's translation added)

> Try this: just fill in the blank.
> Father God, You are _____.
> Lord Creator, You are_____.

I know you are probably thinking, "I'm not so good at this." Well, you *will* get better, I promise.

Glory, it seems, is also a really good New Testament word. We haven't seen many of those kinds of words yet. Look at this verse from Matthew where Jesus is speaking.

> "Let your light shine before men in such a way that they may see your good works and glorify your Father who is in heaven." (Matthew 5:16, NASB95)

Exactly how would this work? Let's say I do something enlightening for Christ. You and some others see it, and you're so inspired that you would glorify your Father who is in heaven. What, specifically, would that look like?

Well, it's probably not as mystical as it seems. You might just thank God for having led me to be light in a dark world. For bringing that word of encouragement to a friend or sharing the gospel with a lost coworker. You might simply say, "To God be the glory." In other words, "Lord, You get all the recognition, praise, and glory for what we just saw. Although Greg did it, You get the credit, Lord. You get the glory. Greg was serving You when he did it. Thank You."

"To God be the glory." Or just "Glory to God!" These are expressions Christians will say from time to time, but we say them because we are commanded to glorify God. We don't really have a way of increasing God's glory, so we just say it: "To God be the glory!" In your worship time, think of things you have done that might be praiseworthy, and just give God all the praise. Think of something you saw someone else do, that impressed you, something that advanced the kingdom of God, then give God the pats on the back. Tell Him, "Lord, You get all the glory. May You be glorified. To God be the glory!"

> To God be the glory
> Great things He has done
> So loved He the world that He gave us His Son
> Who yielded His life an atonement for sin
> And opened the life-gate that all may go in. [30]

There is one more small subscript to this worship stone that we really should explore. Several times in the scriptures, we saw the phrase, "Glorify His name." Why *His name*? I'm going to fully explore the Names of God in a later chapter. When we get there, remind me to talk about "Glorify His name."

Love

A Pharisee, an expert in the Mosaic law, asked Jesus this question:

> "'Teacher, which is the great commandment in the Law?' And He said to him,
> "'You shall love the Lord your God with all your heart, and with all your
> soul, and with all your mind.' This is the great and foremost commandment.
> The second is like it, 'You shall love your neighbor as yourself.' On these
> two commandments depend the whole Law and the Prophets." (Matthew
> 22:36–40, NASB95)

No one would argue that LOVE should be the central motivator in all our relationships. To say, "I love my wife and children" brings to mind a clear picture to most of us. Love is a universal concept that I could never explain in these pages. Love is an "intense feeling of deep affection;" it's an emotion, an interest, and a pleasure. Yet, with all these words, love is still really hard to define, so let's don't. Instead, let's just use things that we know love is, and put them into our worship. It pleases a spouse to hear you say it. "I love you," and it pleases your Heavenly Father to hear you say it as well. "Father, I love You."

The Aramaic family name for father in New Testament times was "Abba." Today, a small Israeli child might call his father, "Abba." So, in your most intimate and familiar time of worship, you might say, "Abba, I love you."

You have heard me refer to my earthly father as "Daddy." He was never (rarely) one to tell us boys that he loved us, and we rarely ever said it back. It was different, I'm sure, for my older sister. He showed us his love in a thousand ways, and we showed our love for him as well. But, late in his life, as his breath began to fail him, he would whisper to me, "Son, I love you." And in return…"I love you too, Daddy." We shared these intimate moments many times toward the end of his life. But now I have wished a million times that I had told him this more as a younger man. I wish we had expressed this sooner, because it meant so much to me when we did finally say it, out loud, to each other. Now, in my private worship of my Heavenly Father, I am liberal with "Abba, I love You."

LOVE, no doubt, is a verb that must have actions to go along with the feelings. But there is no more effective way to show your LOVE than to simply, and sincerely, say it.

Practice that right now. Say this out loud:

"Jesus, I love You."

"I love You, Jesus."

"Father, I love You with all my heart."

"I love You, Holy Spirit."

It's good to hear yourself say something that may be new to you. Practice telling Abba you love Him.

Praise – Hallelujah – HALLEL Yahweh

> "Enter His gates with thanksgiving <u>And His courts with praise</u>. Give thanks to Him, bless His name. For the Lord is good; His lovingkindness is everlasting And His faithfulness to all generations." (Psalm 100:4–5, NASB95)

PRAISE is an expression of approval or admiration. But the expression of "Praise the Lord!" has become overused. Anyone might say, "Praise the Lord" light-heartedly (or even as a way of mocking a Christian). In the same way, "Hallelujah" has become a word for the world to hijack for its own purposes. I've heard people say "Hallelujah!" just as a way of exclaiming their happiness or good fortune. It's become "one of those words," and I doubt that many people really know what they're saying when they use the word in vain. In fact, if you Google the word, a very popular song written by Leonard Cohen, a well-known Canadian song writer, comes up. It starts out pretty good as a ballad about King David. It tells the story of Bathsheba and how she beguiled the king. Then it turns into a song about the difficulties of love. And the song ends with these lines:

> And it's not a cry that you hear at night
> It's not somebody who's seen the light
> It's a cold and it's a broken Hallelujah.
> Hallelujah, Hallelujah [31]

This is one of the most recorded and covered songs of all time by various artists and languages. *Hallelujah* has become a very popular word.

HALLELUJAH is a Hebrew word straight from the scriptures, a compound word made up of "*HALLELU*" and "*YAH*." *HALLELU* is an exhortation to a group of people to praise something or someone: you *all* praise. *YAH* is the shortened version of Yahweh, the covenant name of God. We will learn about this name in <u>Names of God</u> later. So, you can think of hallelujah as an exhortation to more than one person to praise Yahweh! It's an admonition for others to sing or say joyous boasts to God.[15] (If you are confused about Y and J, read <u>Wave to Jay</u> in the <u>Appendix</u>. After you read it you might still be confused.)

We can easily criticize non-believers for misusing this wonderful word but, in truth, so do we. If I simply said to God, "Hallelujah!," then what I am actually doing is exhorting the Trinity to give a joyous praise to Yahweh. Technically, it is more appropriate for a worship leader to shout *Hallelujah*! to the worshipers in church. If I wanted to praise God in the Hebrew language, I might better say, "*HALLEL YHWH*! Praise Yahweh!"

This Hebrew word appears in the Bible 24 times from Psalms 104-150. If you look for it, you'll never find it because our English Bibles translate it as *"Praise the LORD!"* (as in Psalm 106:1). The *King James Version* actually translates it most accurately as "Praise ye the LORD!" You praise the LORD! The psalmist is exhorting us to PRAISE the LORD!

I know it seems like I may have ruined this great word for us all. But let me assure you that if you want to shout HALLELUJAH! at the top of your lungs in true and passionate praise to our God, then I really doubt He will be as picky about the etymology of the word as I am. If by saying hallelujah you are giving praise to God, then keep it up.

But, is our just *saying* "Praise God" actually praising God? Maybe, maybe not. If your 12-year-old daughter had the lead role in a school musical and got a standing ovation, would you run up to her after the show and say, "Praise you, Daughter!?" No way! You would jump around and hug her and tell her that she was so good, and that her diction was perfect, and her dance was the best ever!

When it comes time to PRAISE God, then really PRAISE Him.
"Father God, You are great and powerful and awesome in creation."
"You are loving and gracious and kind in your dealings with me."

Like thanksgiving, praise can go on forever. Let it. God deserves all the PRAISE you can ever give Him. Be as specific as you can. You are extolling God for His character, His nature, His righteousness, His lovingkindness, and His justice. You are praising God and He likes it. It pleases Him. So, my best advice to you regarding PRAISING God is this: HALLELUJAH!

Prayer

PRAYER can certainly be part of worship, and it may seem even to be the most integral part of worship. But we can pray and not worship. And we can worship and not pray. PRAYER can be structured if you like that approach, or PRAYER can be freeform if that suits you better. You might even do both, from one time to another. I'm not here to teach you about prayer; I will leave that to E.M. Bounds or Philip Yancey. But let's just consider prayer as conversation with God. It is personal and intimate, or it can be public and shared. Prayer is a two-way conversation between you and your Maker. But one thing it should never be is just a one-way list of your needs and desires.

Supplication (asking God to supply your needs) is part of prayer, but only part. If you are going to pray, I recommend you start with some PRAISE. Simply recognize who God is and what He means to you, just in that moment. Make sure your sins are current. If there are unconfessed sins, then confess them. Be specific. Express to God what you intend to do about them. *Repent*, and be specific. Then *Ask*. Make your requests known to God. He loves you and wants you to ask. All sorts of scriptures come to mind here, but I'll resist the urge to preach. Lastly is *Yield*. Put your whole self before God and give Him access to everything you are and have and want. Say YES! to anything He wants.

And, there's your acrostic. **P**raise – **R**epent – **A**sk – **Y**ield.

Praying can be a critical STONE in your worship altar as you just talk to God and listen to what He says. But we can describe worship in the same way. Our worship is an intimate time of personal interaction and reflection with the creator of the universe.

> "Rejoice always, pray without ceasing, give thanks in all circumstances; for this is the will of God in Christ Jesus for you." (1 Thess. 5:16–18, ESV)

> "And when you pray, do not heap up empty phrases as the Gentiles do, for they think that they will be heard for their many words. Do not be like them, for your Father knows what you need before you ask him." (Matthew 6:7–8, ESV)

Proclaim - Ascribe

To PROCLAIM is to make a public announcement of some importance.

To ASCRIBE is to attribute a quality as belonging to someone.

These words can be used in other situations with different definitions. But, for the context of worshiping God, these meanings will do. Let's go back to the example of praising a child for a good performance in dance or a good cheerleading competition. I might say out loud to her dance instructor, "Katie really did well with her fouetté turns." Or, of Emily, I might tell her how disciplined she was in the cheer stunts while holding up the flier. (These are my two daughters, and I was a dance/cheer Dad. So, I have some real-sounding examples.) I *proclaimed* the quality of Katie's turns, and I *ascribed* strength to Emily's job as a base. I just want you to see here, in my worship, that I might PROCLAIM some quality of God. I might say it out loud to others in a public setting, or I might say it directly to God Himself in my private setting. I might also ASCRIBE a quality to God that I have seen in Him in my own life.

Here are a few examples from scripture.

> "For I proclaim the name of the LORD; Ascribe greatness to our God! The Rock! His work is perfect, for all His ways are just; A God of faithfulness and without injustice, Righteous and upright is He." (Deuteronomy 32:3–4, NASB95)

> "The LORD is my light and my salvation; Whom shall I fear? The LORD is the defense of my life; Whom shall I dread?" (Psalm 27:1, NASB95)

> "I love You, O LORD, my strength. The LORD is my rock and my fortress and my deliverer, My God, my rock, in whom I take refuge; My shield and the horn of my salvation, my stronghold. I call upon the LORD, who is worthy to be praised, And I am saved from my enemies." (Psalm 18:1–3, NASB95)

At times David speaks to God directly (in first-person attribution) and, at other times, he speaks about God in the second person (proclamation).

In my time of worship, I might ASCRIBE or attribute a quality to God. "Lord, You are my provider. Your generosity through my job amazes me."

But in speaking to another person, I might PROCLAIM something about God. So, I can worship God in a setting where I'm talking with another person. If a person tells me I am a good provider for my family, then I might say to them, "The Lord gives me the ability to work and provide for my family. Everything we have comes from Him." I'm PROCLAIMING God's praise, and that is worship.

We can worship God in our church setting and our private setting, but we can also worship God in any public setting when we give Him praise for who He is and what He has done for us.

There are those predictable phrases like, "Praise the Lord!" and "To God be the glory." These will do in a pinch. But think up your own responses that reflect God in your own life. If you get a compliment for some skill, you might say, "God has been good to me." If someone asks you a tough life question, you might respond with, "Well, the Bible says, 'All things work for good for those who love the Lord.'" You can worship God in any life situation if you are just aware and *ready to do so*. Your whole life can reflect not only what God has done for you, but who God is. Your life can be a proclamation! If your responses are too canned or trite, you might have a negative effect on people. Let your worship be a natural part of how you interact with people. Sincere, not overbearing, or pious, simply reflecting to others the Holy Spirit who lives in you.

Practice this in private. Write down a few phrases below that sound like you. Try them out on your spouse or Christian friends. Then, when it happens for real, your words will just come out as a natural part of the conversation. Afterward just say directly to God, "Thank You, Lord. That was for You." And *that* was worship as well.

_____

_____

_____

_____

_____

_____

_____

_____

Raising Hands

– and other postures.

I was raised in the Methodist church in rural Georgia so, for us, worship in church was pretty tame. We sang out of the *Cokesbury Hymnal*, and we stood when the preacher read from the big gold-leaf King James that was always open on the pulpit. Every Sunday, we recited

> *Worship is the highest elevation of the spirit, and yet the lowliest prostration of the soul.*
>
> – CHARLES H. SPURGEON

the Apostles Creed, "I believe in God, the Father Almighty, Creator of Heaven and earth…" One thing we never did as Methodists was raise our hands in worship. In fact, we usually sat on our hands.

I had an uncle who was a suspected Pentecostal. He might say "Amen" on occasion, but that was about the extent of it. I married a Baptist, so we joined a Southern Baptist Church. For only the second time in my life, I saw people raise their hands in church. (The first time was a different story I'll tell you another time.) Hand-raising made me uncomfortable at first. But then, as teachers of a college Sunday school class, Vicki and I visited a charismatic church for a concert. Oh boy! People not only raised their hands, but they raised everything else. They jumped and danced and shouted. They spoke in tongues. It was a Holy Spirit party, and I was clearly there by mistake. In the years since, I've explored just about every style of church worship there is and, I have to say, if you believe it pleases God and you can show me some scriptural backing, then I say, "Go for it." Everyone will find their comfort zone with worship. Some will be more demonstrative in their worship, others more stoic. I imagine that most Christians will find themselves someplace happily in the middle. Your personality will dictate how you express yourself in life and in worship. No matter where you find your sweet spot, if God is glorified and you find joy, then you should never feel ashamed of how you worship God in church.

In 2 Samuel, King David famously "danced before the Lord with all his might" at the return of the Ark of the Covenant. He wore nothing but a linen ephod, a priestly garment that evidently didn't cover everything. His wife, Michal, scorned him for being so shameless and foolish. David was rather pleased with his expression of worship because it was between him and his God.

I guess the lesson here is that we might want to dance in worship, or we might not. Some churches do and some don't. But, either way, we should find our worship lane and not criticize others when they find theirs.

What about private worship? Remember that your attitudes are important in worship, and an attitude is an idea that's expressed in your actions. Look at it this way: if you were a little child and missed your daddy who's been away, then when he comes home you are likely to throw your hands up toward Him. You might jump and dance around. This response speaks volumes to your father about what you feel and want. So, if you are seeking your Heavenly Father in private worship and it seems meaningful to throw your hands up and dance around, then do it. If it feels right to KNEEL, then kneel. Maybe you need to be flat on your face in SUBMISSION or CONFESSION. Your actions and posture will speak to God in ways that words can never express.

> "Hear the voice of my supplications when I cry to You for help, When I lift
> up my hands toward Your holy sanctuary." (Psalm 28:2, NASB95)

Your RAISED HANDS or body posture should never focus attention on yourself. Never be a distraction to other worshipers. If you feel that raising your hands in church brings the attention of others to you, then don't do it. When we worship God, all our attention should be FOCUSED on Him and never ourselves.

> "Ezra opened the book in the sight of all the people for he was standing above
> all the people; and when he opened it, all the people stood up. Then Ezra
> blessed the LORD the great God. And all the people answered, 'Amen, Amen!'
> while lifting up their hands; then they bowed low and worshiped the LORD
> with their faces to the ground." (Nehemiah 8:5–6, NASB95)

Read

I've been a Bible teacher for most of my adult life. That may sound impressive but it's not. When I was in my 20s, my friend, Tony, told me I was going to co-teach a young adult Sunday School class with him. I told him no, I'm not. He said, oh, yes you are. And that was that! I had never taught anyone anything. (I did teach my little brother how to cuss once, which didn't turn out so well.)

> It is the pleasing of God that is at the heart of worship. Therefore, our worship must be informed at every point by the Word of God as we seek God's own instructions for worship that is pleasing to Him.
>
> —R.C. Sproul

Every other Sunday, I had to stand up in front of a bunch of smart college kids and teach them the Bible. I was terrified. But I realized that if I was going to teach it, I had better learn it. So, I did. To learn it, I had to read it and then read it some more. That experience began a life-long love affair with God's Word. I have taught adult Bible study on and off for most of the 40 years since. I learned that I could make a complex topic sound simple. I guess if you do anything long enough, you can't help but get good at it. This learned skill translated over into my work life, and I was able to make a career of it as well. I explained technology to non-technical people. Again, if you do anything long enough...

When you stand up in front of a group of people and attempt to teach them something, you hope for some kind of positive feedback. Maybe a "nice job," or "I enjoyed that," is about all you can really expect. (A standing O is just not in the cards.) Occasionally, however, over these many years of teaching, I have gotten the ultimate compliment from a listener. Someone will quote me. They will say back to me something I taught them before. They were actually listening! Wow!

I've taught a particular lesson many times about how we become more like Jesus. It involves a tree and an arrow. One Sunday morning not long ago, a young man from my mentoring group came to me, rolled up his shirt sleeve, and showed me his tattoo. It was the tree and the arrow.

The highest praise for a teacher or author is for someone to repeat back to them something they have said. In my worship, from time to time, I will just read back to God something He wrote for me.

"How blessed is the man who does not walk in the counsel of the wicked, nor stand in the path of sinners, Nor sit in the seat of scoffers! But his delight is in the law of the LORD, And in His law, he meditates day and night. He will be like a tree firmly planted by streams of water, which yields its fruit in its season and its leaf does not wither; and in whatever he does, he prospers." (Psalm 1:1–3, NASB95)

"Lord, that man is me. My delight is in Your words. I am Your tree, firmly planted by streams of water. Thank You." I just say back to God what He has said to me, what He has instilled in my heart.

READING God's Word as part of our worship in church is a common practice. We might even stand together in honor of His Word as a pastor reads aloud. I have learned to do it in my private worship as well, and I encourage you to do the same. It takes a little preparation. During your personal Bible study, put together a list of scripture references that are especially meaningful to you. They don't necessarily have to be "worship" scriptures. During your private worship, pull out your Bible, find one of these scriptures, and just READ it out loud to God. He is the author, after all, and He will be pleased with your effort. Remember: it's one of the greatest compliments for a teacher to hear his student read back to him something he wrote. Something meaningful, impactful, and that made a difference in the student's life.

OK, ready to step it up a notch? *Quote God's Word from memory*, right back to Him. Reading from an author's work is one thing, but memorizing it takes it to a whole new level. That's the greatest compliment of all.

Complimenting God for something He has done is what worship is all about, don't you think? And a tattoo? You can decide.

Rejoice

"Rejoice in the Lord always; again I will say, rejoice!" (Phil.4:4, NASB95)

Who doesn't want to REJOICE? It's happy and exuberant and full of joy! But there needs to be a pretty convincing reason for that much delight. And exactly what does REJOICE look like? How do you show great joy?

I guess the answer is…I don't exactly know, but I know it when I feel it. REJOICE is a feeling of sheer delight. It almost always involves an uncontrollable smile. It might even include hugs and a high-five. OK, so how do you "high-five" God? REJOICE.

Maybe rejoicing also includes giving joy to someone else. Rejoicing is something we should do together. [Also see Delight.]

Christmas morning has always been a special time at our house. Vicki and I have raised two girls, and we have always had Christmas traditions that we just don't forget. One of those traditions is that we wrap all the presents and open them on Christmas morning. There is nothing so wonderful as a little girl tearing open the paper and seeing the American Girl doll she has asked for. Smiles, and hugs, and more hugs. That's what "REJOICE" looks like.

"Rejoice in the Lord always…"

When I think about what Jesus has done for me…when I consider the price He paid… when I see Him risen up all glorious and shining…when I picture Him on His throne, taking up my case before the Father…when I think about all this, then I can't help but smile. I want to hug Him forever! *That's* what REJOICE looks like. Sometimes REJOICE looks like uncontrollable tears when I find myself in His presence – before His throne – filled with His love, weeping for joy.

As you rise up each morning and tear the paper off a new day, as you see the new mercies He has prepared for you today, declare that "this is the day my Yahweh has made for me. I will rejoice and be glad in it."

> "But let the righteous be glad; let them exult before God; Yes, let them rejoice with gladness. Sing to God, sing praises to His name; Lift up a song for Him who rides through the deserts, whose name is the LORD, and exult before Him." (Psalm 68:3–4, NASB95)

Remember

"Bless the LORD, O my soul, And all that is within me, bless His holy name.
Bless the LORD, O my soul, And forget none of His benefits;
Who pardons all your iniquities,
Who heals all your diseases,
Who redeems your life from the pit,
Who crowns you with lovingkindness and compassion,
Who satisfies your years with good things, So that your youth is renewed
like the eagle.
The LORD performs righteous deeds and judgments for all who are oppressed.
He made known His ways to Moses, His acts to the sons of Israel.
The LORD is compassionate and gracious, Slow to anger and abounding in
lovingkindness.
He will not always strive with us, nor will He keep His anger forever.
He has not dealt with us according to our sins, nor rewarded us according
to our iniquities.
For as high as the heavens are above the earth, so great is His lovingkindness
toward those who fear Him.
As far as the east is from the west, so far has He removed our transgressions
from us.
Just as a father has compassion on his children, So the LORD has compassion
on those who fear Him."
(Psalm 103:1–13, NASB95)

"And forget none of His benefits…"

That's an amazing and simple sentence of scripture with a double negative of sorts. So, let's turn it around and say it this way: "REMEMBER all the good things that God has done for me." It might be a worthwhile exercise at some point to make a physical list. Try to write down ALL the good things God has done for you. If you are anything like me, this would be an impossible task, but worth a try anyway. That's what David began to do in this wonderful song #103. David says, "Let's REMEMBER what God has done for us. He pardons, heals, redeems, crowns, satisfies, renews, blesses, and teaches. He is compassionate, gracious, patient, loving, and forgiving." One of my favorite Old Testament words is "lovingkindness." It's the Hebrew word, *CHESED*. Forget the C and pronounce it like HAY'-SED, putting emphasis on the first syllable. OK, now try to clear your throat as if you had to spit. KKKHHH. Now say it. KKKHHHAY' SED. If word origin is not your thing, then that's OK. The English word is beautiful enough. I want to remember that God, my Father, crowns me with lovingkindness and compassion. Picture *that* in your mind. He "crowns" me with His lovingkindness and His compassion. He satisfies my years (my desires) with good things. And as I am REMINDED of these things, then all I want to do is bless Him, praise Him, thank Him. Worship Him.

Think of the very best things God has done for you:

_____

_____

_____

_____

_____

_____

_____

_____

_____

_____

_____

_____

_____

_____

_____

Rest

"You can rest when you're dead. Get back to work!"

> *Just as your body needs sleep, your soul needs time to rest in God.*
> – CRAIG GROESCHEL

I know that a lot of people have this attitude. "I don't have time to rest. There is just too much to do." If you are part of a family with young kids, believe me, I understand your situation. But I don't need to nag anyone about getting some rest. Your body will simply demand it, and you will finally sit down.

But the type of rest I'm talking about in this book is not the kind of rest needed for the weary of body and mind. Certainly, this kind of rest *is* needed and prescribed to us by God.

> "Remember the sabbath day, to keep it holy. Six days you shall labor and do
> all your work, but the seventh day is a sabbath of the LORD your God; in it
> you shall not do any work…" (Exodus 20:8–10, NASB95)

REST for the weary will indeed bring a recovery of strength and a rejuvenation of the soul. But in our worship, we must be able to rest in the Lord with a kind of REST taught to us by King David.

> "Do not fret because of evildoers,
> Be not envious toward wrongdoers.
> For they will wither quickly like the grass and fade like the green herb.
> Trust in the LORD and do good; Dwell in the land and cultivate faithfulness.
> Delight yourself in the LORD; And He will give you the desires of your heart.
> Commit your way to the LORD, Trust also in Him, and He will do it.
> He will bring forth your righteousness as the light and your judgment as the
> noonday.
> Rest in the LORD and wait patiently for Him;
> Do not fret because of him who prospers in his way, Because of the man who
> carries out wicked schemes.
> Cease from anger and forsake wrath;
> Do not fret; it leads only to evildoing. For evildoers will be cut off,
> But those who wait for the LORD, they will inherit the land." (Psalm 37:1–9,
> NASB95)

In this worship song, David encourages his worshipers to REST – not only from physical labors – but from emotional and mental stress. He says again and again, "Do not fret – do not be envious – do not fret – cease from anger – forsake wrath." Instead, he tells us to "trust – delight – commit – rest in the Lord and wait patiently for Him." RESTING in the Lord, it seems, is about *releasing our anxiety and stress found in dealing with the wickedness of the world*. About setting these things aside as we worship Him. Replacing them with trust, delight, and commitment. If we learn to "REST in the Lord and wait patiently for Him," we will "inherit the land." We will receive God's best for us, as His heirs and children.

Most days we carry around with us something that someone else has done to us or others. Something hurtful, something threatening, something evil. Problems with family relationships can be the most hurtful and damaging things we bear. They can range from a harsh word to a threat to an act of aggression. We might be concerned for the wellbeing of a child or a spouse. We would do anything just to lay down these burdens, even if just for an hour, and find some PEACE from them.

Worship is the perfect place to do just that. As we enter into His presence, we might just lay down these burdens, placing them on the altar before the Lord. I know this idea is a mental and verbal exercise, but to release our fretting and anger and worry before the Lord is a real and precious act of SACRIFICE. Your Father is not bothered by your burdens; He welcomes them.

> "Therefore, humble yourselves under the mighty hand of God, that He may exalt you at the proper time, casting all your anxiety on Him, because He cares for you." (1 Peter 5:6–7, NASB95)

> "Rejoice in the Lord always; again, I will say, rejoice! Let your gentle spirit be known to all men. The Lord is near. <u>Be anxious for nothing</u>, but in everything by prayer and supplication with thanksgiving let your requests be made known to God. And the peace of God, which surpasses all comprehension, will guard your hearts and your minds in Christ Jesus. Finally, brethren, whatever is true, whatever is honorable, whatever is right, whatever is pure, whatever is lovely, whatever is of good repute, if there is any excellence and if anything, worthy of praise, dwell on these things. The things you have learned and received and heard and seen in me, practice these things, and the God of peace will be with you." (Philippians 4:4–9, NASB95)

Say out loud the things that burden you, that cause you anxiety. Say to the Lord of

Heaven, "I lay these burdens at Your feet." Then lay them down as you would take off an old coat and place it on the ground. You don't have to spell them out or go into any detail. He knows exactly what burdens you. He just wants to see and hear you put them down. He cares and wants to see you freed from them. Put them down.

Then, put on the new garment of PRAISE. Tell God something that is true and honorable about the source of your distress. Think of something that is right and pure and lovely. Say something good about the person who has caused you pain. Speak well of them to God. Anything that is excellent or worthy of praise, dwell on these things before your Lord.

The result is the peace of God. A peace that is beyond our understanding that will guard and protect our hearts and minds. And this peace comes to us through our Cornerstone, Jesus Christ.

> "Come to Me, all who are weary and heavy-laden, and I will give you rest. Take My yoke upon you and learn from Me, for I am gentle and humble in heart, and YOU WILL FIND REST FOR YOUR SOULS. For My yoke is easy and My burden is light." (Matthew 11:28–30, NASB95)

Seek

To "seek" sounds like we are looking for something, to attempt, or to achieve a goal. We might seek something we desire. Or we might just ask for something from someone. Two scriptures come to mind:

> "Seek the LORD while He may be found; Call upon Him while He is near." (Isaiah 55:6, NASB95)

> "Ask, and it will be given to you; seek, and you will find; knock, and it will be opened to you." (Matthew 7:7, NASB95)

Yes, we can seek blessings and provision from the Lord, but *this* SEEK is different. Many times in scripture we are told to "Seek God's face."

> "When You said, 'Seek My face,' my heart said to You, 'Your face, O LORD, I shall seek.'" (Psalm 27:8, NASB95)

Does God have a face? The Hebrew word for "face" in the Old Testament is often translated "presence." When we seek the face of God, we are seeking His presence. Our worship time is "before the Father," in His presence. If we are going to *be* in His presence, at times we must seek it. At times we may be close to God, and at other times we may be further away. Maybe we have been fleshly or selfish or sinful in some way. Maybe we have slipped away from God.

As I set aside a time for worship, can I just assume He is there waiting for me? Well, yes and no. God is always close, as close as His Spirit who dwells inside you. But if He *seems* not-so-close, He didn't move; you did. So, SEEK the Lord. SEEK His face, up close and personal. Desire God's intimate presence. Call out to Him. If there is sin, CONFESS it. If there is doubt, set that aside. God wants you to be in His close presence, but you must leave your sins at the door.

Ask, seek, and knock. These were the words of Jesus. We can apply them to many areas of life, but worship is a perfect place to ask for God's approval, SEEK His presence, and knock for access.

> "Now set your heart and your soul to seek the LORD your God;" (1 Chronicles 22:19, NASB95)

Silence

"My soul waits in silence for God only; From Him is my salvation. He only is my rock and my salvation, My stronghold; I shall not be greatly shaken." (Psalm 62:1–2, NASB95)

"My soul, wait in silence for God only, For my hope is from Him. He only is my rock and my salvation, My stronghold; I shall not be shaken. On God my salvation and my glory rest; The rock of my strength, my refuge is in God.

Trust in Him at all times, O people; Pour out your heart before Him; God is a refuge for us." (Psalm 62:5–8, NASB95)

Fred Rogers was and is an American icon. He hosted his TV show, *Mister Rogers' Neighborhood*, on PBS from 1969 to 1975, and again from 1978 to 2001. It's one of the longest-running children's TV shows, second only to *Sesame Street*. Mr. Rogers was a Presbyterian minister with a quiet, measured voice and a manner that put everyone at ease. He died in 2003 at age 74. He is famous for the question, "Would you be my neighbor?", as well as for a few simple little songs and, of course, his cardigan and blue sneakers. But there was one practice he saved for adults, his one minute of silence.

Mr. Rogers gave the 2002 commencement address at Dartmouth College. Here is a bit of his speech…

"I'd like to give you all an invisible gift. A gift of a silent minute to think about those who have helped you become who you are today. Some of them may be here right now. Some may be far away. Some, like my astronomy professor, may even be in heaven. But wherever they are, if they've loved you, and encouraged you, and wanted what was best in life for you, they're right inside yourself. And I feel that you deserve quiet time, on this special occasion, to devote some thought to them. So, let's just take a minute, in honor of those that have cared about us all along the way. One silent minute…"

And so, they did. You can watch the speech on *YouTube*. That minute, to those students and their families, I'm sure was interminable. But boy was it powerful!

Let's try this for ourselves, right now. When I say "go," we are going to sit in silence for one minute. I want you to think about the people who have helped make you who you are today. Think about those who loved you into this world and those who have encouraged you along the way. (Set a timer on your phone.)

Ready? OK, go.

. . . .

Thank you.

A minute is a long time, and just a moment. If I microwave my oatmeal for a minute, it flies by. If I'm pressing hard for the final 60 seconds in my cycling class, a minute seems like an eternity. But both are exactly the same.

Now add silence to the minute and it changes everything.

There is power in silence.[16]

The psalmist, at first, tells us, "My soul waits in silence for God only." My soul. We are three parts: body, soul, and spirit. Our soul is also three parts: *mind* (what we think), *emotions* (what we feel), and *will* (what we desire). My thoughts, my feelings, and my desires all go on hold; they wait in SILENCE. And this SILENCE is a tribute to Elohim alone because He is my rock, my salvation, my stronghold. Only He deserves this silent soul-waiting. Because of Him, "I shall not be greatly shaken."

Later, the psalmist changes perspective. He *instructs* his soul to wait. "My soul, wait in silence for God only." This time his reasons are given: "My hope is from Him. He is my rock, my salvation, my stronghold, I shall not be shaken. My salvation and glory all depend on Him. He is the rock of my strength; He is my refuge." He instructs his readers (that's us) to "trust in Him at all times. Pour out your heart before Him; God is a refuge for us."

We all have just such a list of who and what God is to us. Things we want to ACKNOWLEDGE about God. Things we want to THANK Him for and PRAISE Him for. Before we say this list out loud, let me encourage you to give Him an offering of SILENCE. It is an act of worship. Just wait before Him and think of Him. Think of Abba and His lovingkindness for you. Think of Jesus and His amazing words of HOPE. Think of the PEACE that Holy Spirit brings, seals you in, and promises.

> "Finally, brethren, whatsoever things are <u>true</u>, whatsoever things are <u>honest</u>, whatsoever things are <u>just</u>, whatsoever things are <u>pure</u>, whatsoever things are <u>lovely</u>, whatsoever things are of <u>good report</u>; if there be any <u>virtue</u>, and if there be any <u>praise</u>, think on these things." (Philippians 4:8, KJV)

GREG DIXON

Think on these things. If you just sit unguarded in silence, then *your* earthly thoughts, feelings, and desires will crowd out the silence. So set these things aside, just for a time, and think on these *good* things. This mental discipline will take some practice, but it is well worth it. WAIT in SILENCE before God.

There is power in silence.
Just ask Mr. Rogers.

[See also Wait and Listen.]

Sing

"O come, let us sing for joy to the LORD, Let us shout joyfully to the rock of our salvation. Let us come before His presence with thanksgiving, Let us shout joyfully to Him with psalms." (Psalm 95:1–2, NASB95)

> *The gift of language combined with the gift of song was given to man that he should proclaim the Word of God through music.*
> – MARTIN LUTHER

"Shout joyfully to the LORD, all the earth. Serve the LORD with gladness; Come before Him with joyful singing." (Psalm 100:1–2, NASB95)

Some people just have the "gift of gab." They can just talk to anyone about anything at any time. I've always been a bit jealous about this gift, particularly since I was put into situations all throughout my professional career where I was expected to start and lead a conversation with strangers. Just left to my own capabilities, I might do well with the introduction and a handshake; but it's about there that I dry up. I'm just not good at small talk. My wife, Vicki, on the other hand, is naturally gifted at conversation. I listen to her get a conversation started and keep it going, and I'm amazed (and even a little ashamed) that I'm such a dullard!

When we pray together, she can fly from topic to topic with ease while I'm still stuck at "Dear Lord." I'm just not capable of easily starting a conversation, even with God. I can get there, eventually, but I need a little boost.

My private worship is like that, too. I need a plan with a Step 1. Once I get started, I can keep it going with Step 2. So, for me, that's where MUSIC is so valuable. I see worship songs as putting words in my heart that I can't come up with on my own. The lyrics of a good worship song speak directly to God. And if I SING these words in church along with a few hundred other worshipers, then I can be more comfortable with my worship. I'm not a very good singer, so hearing my voice along with all the others makes me feel better about my efforts to sing to God. I SING the words as though they were my own so naturally some songs attract me more than others. Some song lyrics just sound like the words I want to say to God. I guess we all have our favorites.

Singing is and has always been a vital part of corporate worship. Many churches have a choir or worship team who sing and lead the congregation in worship together.

Look at any hymnal and you'll see songs that are hundreds of years old. One of my favorites is *A Mighty Fortress is our God*. It was written by Martin Luther about 1527. Of course, Martin Luther, the great reformer, was German. He composed the words in German:

"Ein feste Burg ist unser Gott." The version we sing in church today was written by Fredric Henry Hedge in 1853. It's not a direct translation, but a paraphrase of the original, and says basically the same thing that Luther's original says but in English verses that rhyme.

> A mighty fortress is our God, a bulwark never failing;
> Our helper He, amid the flood of mortal ills prevailing.
> For still our ancient foe, doth seek to work his woe;
> His craft and power are great, and armed with cruel hate,
> On earth is not his equal. [32]

If you grew up in church like I did, you might be comfortable with a traditional hymnal. If so, then it's a great tool to have handy during your worship time. You can order one online. Find the songs you like, ones that speak directly to God, and mark them somehow. I have a go-to list of worship songs that I know by heart. Here's one.

> Blessed assurance, Jesus is mine;
> Oh, what a foretaste of glory divine!
> Heir of salvation, purchase of God,
> Born of His Spirit, washed in His blood.[33]

I mentioned that I need a worship plan, a Step 1. Many times, this first step is a song. My favorite starter song is one written by Laurie Klein, *I Love You, Lord*. It's one of the most popular and widely recorded songs in all contemporary Christian music. Laurie Klein was not an accomplished song writer. She and her husband lived an austere life in Oregon in the 1970s. Laurie described *I Love You, Lord* as 'a gift from heaven' as the lines flowed effortlessly, one after the other.[17] If you don't know the song, look it up online. You can pick it up easily and learn the music. It only has one verse, but it really speaks what I want to say first to God. Here is the verse:

> I love You, Lord,
> And I lift my voice,
> To worship You, oh my soul, rejoice.
> Take joy, my King, in what you hear,
> May it be a sweet, sweet sound in your ear.[34]

If traditional worship music is a bit too "traditional" for you, then something more contemporary is easy to find. Take note of what you sing in church or hear on Christian radio and find it in the online music streaming service you might use. Most services have "channels" called "Christian" or "Worship." Create a playlist with your go-to songs and just press "shuffle" to start. This will let Holy Spirit choose the songs you use this time. Next time, you'll get a different set. If you like, you might make your own song book with the lyrics. Again, all this music is easy enough to find online.

Keep in mind that your worship time is *your* worship time. The music is for your expression to God. Try not to get caught up in just listening to it yourself. Maybe you should limit your worship MUSIC to one song. Then move on to the next STONE.

Music should be a regular part of your private worship experience. God loves to hear you SING to Him.

> "Sing for joy in the LORD, O you righteous ones; Praise is becoming to the upright. Give thanks to the LORD with the lyre; Sing praises to Him with a harp of ten strings. Sing to Him a new song; Play skillfully with a shout of joy." (Psalm 33:1–3, NASB95)

One more thing. If you are gifted with the ability to play MUSIC then, by all means, do so. Vicki is a gifted pianist. She saw to it that Katie, our older daughter, took piano lessons. I will never forget the pride I felt, sitting in Katie's piano recital, listening to her struggle through *Moonlight Sonata*. She was clearly not the best one to perform that day, but I didn't care. Hearing my Katie play for me was payment enough for all the scales and chords and restarts we endured during her practices at home.

A dad loves to hear his kids play MUSIC for him. If you are musical, then consider where your musical gift came from. Think about all the practices, discipline, and effort that went into developing it, and thank your Abba for this gift. Then play for Him. He will be so proud of you. Of such is worship.

Thank

> "Enter His gates with thanksgiving And His courts with praise. Give thanks to Him, bless His name. For the Lord is good; His lovingkindness is everlasting And His faithfulness to all generations." (Psalm 100:4–5, NASB95)

It is generally accepted that Moses wrote Psalms 90–100. We will talk much about Psalms later, especially Psalm 100. For now, let's just get this picture in our minds. Moses was responsible for the tabernacle. It was the place where the Most High dwelt among His people. The Israelites were commanded to worship Him at this tent of meeting which was surrounded by a sturdy tent wall with a single gate. Just inside the gate was a courtyard where the altar of sacrifice sat. We may have this image of great AWE and REVERENCE upon entering the tabernacle to worship the Most High. But Moses leads us to worship with joyful shouts and singing. We are to enter His gates with thanksgiving and His courts with praise and blessings. Why? "For the Lord is good. His lovingkindness is everlasting, and His faithfulness is to all generations." (NASB95)

Literally, verse 4 tells us to "enter His gates with a thank offering." If saying "thanks" ever gets trite or commonplace in your worship, then step up your "thank yous" to a Thank Offering. Enter the gates of the tabernacle with an offering of thanksgiving. A cornucopia of thankfulness. A bushel basket of gratitude. Just thank Him for LOTS of big and little things, and be sincere.

If there is one word that should proceed all others when we come to worship God, it simply must be THANK YOU. That's two words, but I'm sure you see my point. If I have anything to say to God first, it's THANK YOU. But my THANKSGIVING is not because He is good, but because He is good to me. His lovingkindness has been extended to include me. *ME!* I have seen His faithfulness to me and my family. My "thank you" is not some generality expressed on behalf of us all; it's personal. God is due my THANKS because of what He has done for me. For *me.*

But "thank you" is just the beginning. What do I have to be thankful for?

"THANK You, Lord, for my salvation."
"THANK You, Lord, for forgiving *all* my sins."
"THANK You, Lord, for filling me with Your Holy Spirit."
"THANK You, Lord, for giving me Vicki."
"THANK You, Lord, for Katie and Emily and Chris and little Maren."
"THANK You, Lord, for providing for us all so generously."
"THANK You, Lord, for the promises of Your Word."
"THANK You, Lord, for _____."

As you might imagine, MY thanksgiving can go on for quite some time. I have a LOT to be thankful for. In fact, the list can be so long that I might break it up into categories. Today I'm thankful for family. Tomorrow I'm thankful for resources. The next day for health, the next…

Suffice it to say, the THANKSGIVING stone will have a prominent place in your worship. And in the worship of every Christian.

Wait

I love the movie *Chariots of Fire*. Love it! It's the true story of Eric Liddell, the son of Scottish missionaries to China. He ran for the UK in the 1924 Olympics in Paris. He was fast and he knew it. His sister tried to keep his mind on the work of the mission, but he wanted to run, so he delivered this line to her: "I believe God made me for a purpose, for China; but He also made me fast. And when I run, I feel His pleasure." In Paris, on a Sunday morning when he was supposed to be running in the 100-meter dash, he spoke in church instead. He was favored to win that race, and much national pride was at stake, but he honored the Sabbath more. The man who took his place lost. As Liddell stood in the high altar that morning, he spoke these words which were taken from Isaiah, chapter 40.

> "Behold, the nations are as a drop in a bucket, And are counted as the small dust in the balance: All nations before him are as nothing; And they are counted to him less than nothing, and vanity.
>
> He bringeth the princes to nothing; He maketh the judges of the earth as vanity. Hast thou not known? Hast thou not heard, That the everlasting God, the LORD, The Creator of the ends of the earth, Fainteth not, neither is weary? He giveth power to the faint; And to them that have no strength he increaseth might. But they that wait upon the LORD shall renew their strength; They shall mount up with wings as eagles; They shall run, and not be weary; And they shall walk, and not faint."

That movie was 1981. Ever since, I have been obsessed with one thing from that whole scene, that whole movie. Not the fact that Eric Liddell would not run on Sunday. Not the training, or the strength, nor even flying on eagles' wings. It's one word, actually. WAIT. "Yet, those who wait for the LORD ..." Eric Liddell knew what it meant to *wait* before the Lord.

I am not good at waiting. I have a plan, and I like to get on with it. I like to be on time. I don't like to wait on Vicki to leave for church. In conversations, I sometimes feel that I already know what someone is going to tell me, so I want to move on. But that's me. I'm not good at waiting. Maybe that's why I am so intrigued by this notion of *waiting* on God. And that verse! That verse gets me every time. Who doesn't want to "mount up with wings like eagles?"

To figure out what *waiting* is, I think about what a waiter does. The kind of waiter you might find in a nice restaurant. He stands close by and waits. He is waiting on me; he is watching me and my glass of tea. He is anticipating my every need because this dinner isn't his first time at waiting. He knows what I might want and when I might want it because he knows what people want. He's been well-trained. He is patient though. He is hopeful. He wants to please me, with his service. Why? Because that's his job? No, it's because he wants a good tip. So, he waits. There's a lot to be learned from this waiter.

I've studied this whole notion of WAITING on God. I've looked at all the verses, most of them poetic lines from the Psalms that implore us, *implore me,* to WAIT.

The Bible tells us to wait on God 24 times. Most of the time, a worship leader/ psalmist or Old Testament prophet is exhorting us to WAIT on the LORD. As I look at these 24 verses, I can see (by using my Bible study software) that there are five different Hebrew words that we translate as wait. Here they are: *QAVAH – DAMAN – YACHAL – SABAR – CHAKAH.*

Yet, "wait" is a common word used in lots of other biblical contexts besides waiting on God. In these places, these same five words are translated with various nuances. Here are a few of these translations:

- Wait expectantly, wait hopefully, wait eagerly
- Wait in silence, be silent, be still, relax, rest
- Have hope, wait patiently, look, long for

Hebrew is an ancient language with many more shades of meaning to communicate than our modern English language. These nuances are why I like to study the words in the Bible; as I do, *wait* takes on so much more meaning.

As I WAIT *on* God in my worship, I WAIT *before* God. I am in His presence, and I have come to Him to express His worth to me. Perhaps I have told Him of my love, my praise, and my thanks. I have confessed and repented of anything that may hinder my worship. I have blessed and glorified Him. I have asked for some things from Him. I am looking for His guidance or a clear word on a decision. Maybe, now, it's time to wait. So, I WAIT. But what have I learned about waiting? I WAIT in SILENCE. I take a deep cleansing breath; I get still and relax. I rest my body, but not my mind. (Sometimes rest can turn into a nap). I consider the things I have spoken to my Father in worship. I let those things settle in my mind. I examine my motives. Am I satisfied that God is in His place and I am in mine? Will He be lifted up by my desires, or will I? I am waiting, but hopeful and expectant. I want to be patient. I want to hear from God. So, I WAIT. I know He does not speak in a loud voice but in still quiet words – perceptions and heart strings – thoughts and images – memories and notions. I WAIT. My heart longs for Him, for His attention, comfort, and love. I am attentive to Him, not lazy. I stay close, not drifting. *I listen carefully* and resist thoughts that would pull me away, back to the urgent. I WAIT before Him, in His presence, ever listening.

This time of WAITING may be the time that God speaks, so have your pencil and notebook close by. But it more often may be a time of simple sacrifice. A time just to WAIT before your creator and be in His presence. Time is precious, and we would only SACRIFICE to Him an OFFERING which is costly to us and worthy of His attention.

"My soul, wait in silence for God only, For my hope is from Him. He only is my rock and my salvation, My stronghold; I shall not be shaken." (Psalm 62:5–6, NASB95)

"And now, Lord, for what do I wait? My hope is in You." (Psalm 39:7, NASB95)

"You are my hiding place and my shield; I wait for Your word." (Psalm 119:114, NASB95)

"I rise before dawn and cry for help; I wait for Your words." (Psalm 119:147, NASB95)

[See also Silence.]

6

ACKNOWLEDGEMENTS
FOR WORSHIP

Acknowledgement is the acceptance or recognition of something that is true. To "acknowledge" is to show I have "knowledge" of something. I know it and accept it as being completely true.

> *We worship whom we trust, and we trust whom we know.*
>
> – DAVID JEREMIAH

We have established that we must have certain **attitudes** before and during our worship of God. These attitudes put us in the proper state of mind for worship. Next, we discussed **acts** of worship, things we can do that will honor and please God. Again, this a not comprehensive list, but it gives us some STONES to build with. Now we are ready for **acknowledgements,** things we should know about God and "acknowledge" that we know them.

We know the things God does for us, and we REMEMBER them in worship. This act of remembering can be seen as an acknowledgement of what God does. But now we want to look more at *who* God is. We want to begin to acknowledge His character, His nature, His "worthiness," if you will, of our attentions and surrender. Just *who* is this God who demands my devotion and obedience?

Suppose I asked you to think of the one person in the world whom you know best (other than yourself), then just to tell me *about them.* You might use words like "loving," "kind," "caring," "smart," "outgoing." These words describe this person's character, their personality. They describe "who they are." But what if my question was, "Think of the one person in the world you know best, then tell me *who are they*?" You would probably respond with his or her name. Ask *me* this question and I'd say, "Vicki." If you didn't know Vicki, you might ask, "Who is this Vicki?" And I would say, "Vicki is my wife." Her name has meaning for me. It represents her person, her nature, her character. She is loving, has a servant's heart, and is generous. Her name has meaning to me because I acknowledge these things to be true of Vicki.

So, who is God?

The Name

In modern times, three names have come to determine the identity of a person. Names are *that* important to us. I am Gregory Brent Dixon. I'm named after Gregory Peck, a famous movie star in the 1950s. My mom was a big fan.

> *I must take time to worship the One whose name I bear.*
>
> – Oswald Chambers

Daddy was afraid that "Peck" might incur an unfortunate nickname, so they settled on Brent. Had I been a girl, my name would have been June Allison Dixon (famous female actress). My name, even as an infant, had meaning to my parents. They called me "Greg" because Gregory had too many syllables, I guess. The only time I ever heard my whole name was from Mama. If she said, "Gregory Brent!" then I knew I was in trouble. I believe I am the only Gregory Brent Dixon in the country; I'm certainly the only one on Facebook. In that regard, I suppose I am unique to some degree. But it's *not* my name that makes me so. Add to my name a list of characteristics that define who I really am, and you would get a true one-of-a-kind. You would understand who I am, and who God made me to be.

In biblical times, names had a much greater significance. Today we have a surname, our last name that is common to all our immediate family members. Vicki changed her surname from Williford to Dixon when we got married, a custom of more modern times. Our first name is the key to how we identify ourselves; our middle name is just to help create some uniqueness. In the Bible, we most often see a first name as the *only* name of a person. Many books of the Bible are attributed to their authors or who the book was about (e.g., Nehemiah, Esther, Job). But I'm sure Nehemiah was a fairly common name of the time. It meant "comforted by Yahweh." So, who was the Nehemiah that wrote this book?

"The words of Nehemiah the son of Hacaliah." (Nehemiah 1:1a, NASB95)

You might see this written in Hebrew as *NECHEMYAH BEN CHAKALYAH.* Nechemyah (comforted by Yahweh), followed by ben (son of), then Chakalyah (wait for Yahweh). Of course, you would see it in the Hebrew language and alphabet, written right to left.

This man Nehemiah (as we might pronounce it) is, first, a man of Yahweh. (You can hear the "Yah" at the end). Then, to distinguish him from any other Israelite named Nehemiah, he is called "ben Hacaliah," the Nehemiah that is the son of Hacaliah. THAT Nehemiah. This was how names worked in the Old Testament. In the New Testament, *BEN* became *BAR*, perhaps due to the influences of the Aramaic language. Jesus had a disciple whom He called Peter. But his given name was Simon bar-Jonah, or Simon, the son of Jonah.

Today we have a similar convention with last names. The surname Johnson would find its origins as "son of John." Think of all the names you know that end in "son." I am a Dixon, shortened from Dicson or Dickson. I am Greg, Dick's son. Dick would have been his first and only name. The Dixons originate in Scotland as Dickson. Known as a patronymic name, this kind of name comes from the family patron or father. Some surnames come from the family profession like Smith (blacksmith) or Farmer. Surnames were introduced to the British Isles by the Normans during the 11th century. The Scottish Dixon clan has a coat of arms that signifies their place on the battlefield and in the world. This emblem denotes their character and speaks of their good name. The Dixon Coat of Arms is made unique by three stars on a central shield. (The Trinity perhaps?) Our ancient family motto is *Fortes Fortuna Juvat* (Latin) which means, "Fortune helps the brave." A famous New York Yankee baseball player expressed that same thought this way: "I'd rather be lucky than good." (Lefty Gomez)

If you don't know what a coat of arms looks like, just Google it. Not every family name has one. It's more of a British and European custom.

We can begin to see that names and naming conventions change through the years, and your name is important in determining who you are and how you are received by the world. The naming conventions common in Bible times were extremely important to the culture and the family itself.

> "A good name is to be more desired than great wealth, Favor is better than silver and gold." (Proverbs 22:1, NASB95)

At times, a person's name might be changed to reflect his character or reputation. Jesus acknowledged that Simon bar-Jonah was a strong and determined person; to recognize these qualities, Jesus renamed him "Rock" (*CEPHAS* in Aramaic and *PETROS* in Greek). Today we might call this a nickname, but then it was more serious than just a casual reference.

God appointed a man named Abram, son of Terah, to be the father or originator of His chosen people. Abram means "exalted father." But God changed his name to "Abraham" which means "father of many." This name change was designed not only to give Abram a new identity, but also to acknowledge his place in history in the minds of those who would follow him. To this day, Jews and Arabs alike might call themselves "the children of Abraham." But when God gave him this new name, Abram/Abraham was the father of no one. He and his wife were barren of children. Even though Abram was 99 years old, God could see who Abram was to become and who He intended him to be, and his name should reflect that important promise.

God also changed Abraham's wife Sarai to Sarah, who was now 90 years old. She named their son Isaac, which means "he laughs." This was her response when God told her she would be a mother. Moses's name means "to draw out" (*MOSHE*). It was given to him after he was drawn from the Nile River by the Pharaoh's daughter. Of course, it was Moses who also "drew his people out of Egypt." In the New Testament, an angel told Mary (and later, Joseph) to name their son *YESHUA* (Jesus), which means "to save" or "savior."

> "She will bear a Son; and you shall call His name Jesus, for He will save His people from their sins." (Matthew 1:21, NASB95)

Jacob was third in the patriarchal line of succession after Abraham and Isaac. Jews recognized their forefathers as Abraham, Isaac, and Jacob and later referred to themselves as the "children of Jacob." In Genesis 32, Jacob wrestles with an angel all night long. He manages to prevail in his fight and obtains the blessing he demanded. In the end, stubborn and obstinate Jacob receives a new name – *ISRAEL* – which means "he who wrestles with God." This new name reflects his spiritual struggle and the destiny of an entire people who then were called the "sons of Israel." And today, just Israel.

To give or change a person's name, the giver of the name knows and understands the person to be renamed. Assigning a new name assumes some authority over the person as well. Adam was given the authority to name the animals and rule over them.

Let's go back for a minute and think again about British royalty. Imagine I was an emissary from King Henry VIII to Spain. I have all the papers, stamps, and seals to verify my status as the official English ambassador to Spain. Only Henry had the authority to give me this status. As such, I have *his* authority to speak to the officials of Spain, maybe even King Charles V, *in the name of* King Henry VIII of England. While here in Spain, I can speak almost as if I *were* the King of England because I represent his interests, and my documentation bears his name and official seal.

Consider for a moment, what it means to pray *in the name* of Jesus. We pray to God with Jesus's authority and position and place. When He hears me, He hears Jesus, His Son. Holy Spirit is my seal and the Bible is my documentation.

Stop right now and let that sink in.

Does God have a name? Yes, He does.

When Moses asked God that question, God said, "I'm sending you to rescue my people." Moses replied, "When they ask, whom shall I say sent me?" God said, "Tell them…I AM has sent you." His name in Hebrew is Yahweh – I AM. Pronounce it like YAH – WAY. (Actually, the pronunciation of God's name has been lost to time. You might want to read the article in the Appendix, *Wave to Jay.* It explains the relationship between Y and J, and W and V.)

When we try to Anglicize this Hebrew name, YaHWeH, it becomes Jehovah, a word most Christians are familiar with. It's perfectly fine to refer to God as Jehovah if you like, or you can call Him Yahweh. But be careful! God is the creator of the universe and all that is in it. So, who might have authority over God to give Him a name? No one but God could declare this name for Himself; it is a sacred name! God called it His "*covenant name for all time.*" His covenant was the over-arching agreement between God and His people. As part of this covenant, He gave His people ten commandments they must obey; the one about his name is number three from the King James.

> "Thou shalt not take the name of the Lord thy God in vain; for the Lord will not hold him guiltless that taketh his name in vain." (Exodus 20:7, KJV)

Moses received this command written on a stone tablet by Yahweh Himself. On the stone it would have said, "Thou shalt not take the name of YHWH, thy God, in vain…" Now, of course, this command is in English – and King James English at that! But just know that the word *ADONAI* (Hebrew) or Lord (English) was inserted later by Old Testament writers to replace YHWH. So afraid they might violate this third commandment, they edited the original scriptures. (More on this in a minute.)

To use His name in vain is to speak it falsely or commit evil. As King Henry's ambassador to Spain, I might speak in the name of the king of England while in Spain. But if I went next door to Portugal and tried to do the same thing, they might have me arrested. There, I would be using the king's name in vain.

I must not use the name of God falsely. But I also don't want to use His name frivolously or without good purpose, just to emphasize something, or as a swear.

> "And ye shall not swear by my name falsely, neither shalt thou profane the name of thy God: I am the Lord." (Leviticus 19:12, KJV)

We might think of the word "god" in the context of profanity or swearing today. On TV, a person might use a euphemism to replace the word "god," or even say the word, if they are surprised by something. As children, many of us were taught these euphemisms so we would not violate the third commandment. But is it the word "God" that we should not use in vain? Is "God" really His name? Well, I'm going out on a pretty skinny limb here and say, "No, it is not."

> "I am the LORD (*YHWH*), that is My name; I will not give My glory to another, nor My praise to graven images." (Isaiah 42:8, NASB95 Author's translation added)

I would never diminish the seriousness of misusing God's name. I mean, what part of "Thou shalt not!" do we not understand? His name is holy so we must be respectful of how and when we speak it. He doesn't say *don't* speak it; He says *don't* speak it *in vain*. The Jews took this very seriously, maybe too seriously.

The name YHWH is recorded in the scripture more than 6,800 times; every time, a well-meaning scribe or translator replaced it with the word "*ADONAI*" or in English, "LORD." [See Lord – YHWH – Yahweh - Jehovah in the Appendix for more details.]

Whenever this covenant name came up in the writings of Moses or David or some prophet, the scribe would not even write it down. Instead, he would replace it with another Hebrew word, *ADONAI* (Lord). But Adonai had other uses, so when you look in your Bible and see the word "Lord" (initial cap with lower case following), the text is just talking about some higher person, like master, or even referring to God as our master or lord. If you see the word spelled in ALL CAPS – LORD – then you can know that this name is a replacement word for YHWH. The only exception is when the sentence says, "the Lord, GOD" (Adonai, YHWH). See Isaiah 50:7 for an example.

The Hebrew language is written without vowels and from right to left.

יהוה   **YHWH**

H W H Y

←Biblical Hebrew←   →Latin Script→

A special word describes this special name, *tetragrammaton*. It means "The Four Letters." This is the four-letter biblical name of the God of Israel.

Of course, we English speakers need to buy a couple of vowels, so we add the A and the E and spell it left to right. YaHWeH.

In the original Hebrew manuscripts of the Old Testament, the word YHWH (or "Yahweh") was written as the proper covenant name of God. But so holy was this name, later scribes could not even write it because the reader would have to speak it; and, just by accident, he might use it in vain. Instead, these scribes called him "Lord" (*ADONAI*), "God" (*ELOHIM*), or just "The Name" (*HA-SHEM*).

Our Bibles still reflect this abundance of caution, even today.

Read Psalm 8:9 in most any version and you will see both uses of "lord."

O LORD, our Lord, how majestic is Your name in all the earth! (NASB95)

O YHWH, our Adonai, how majestic is Your name in all the earth!

A great many verses in the Bible point us not to God Himself but to "the *name* of God." Why is this? Why not just refer to God, rather than His name?

"Daniel said, 'Let the name of God be blessed forever and ever, for wisdom and power belong to Him.'" (Daniel 2:20, NASB95)

"I will praise the name of God (*ELOHIM*) with song and magnify Him with thanksgiving." (Psalm 69:30, NASB95 Author's translation added)

King David fully understood that the generic Hebrew word for "god" was *EL*. This name could be used to describe any of the gods people worshiped at the time. However, as David wrote a worship song like Psalm 69, the name of El (God) represented to him the nature and character of the *God he knew* and worshiped, not simply a generic god. To demonstrate this understanding, David called Him "Elohim," not "El." Elohim is the plural form of El. Perhaps David used this form to magnify the qualities of El. Maybe he wanted to separate Elohim from other false gods. Christians tend to believe that this speaks of the triune nature of the Father, Son, and Holy Spirit. Three in One. Of course, the Trinity is more fully developed in the New Testament. So even this more generic word "God," as His name in scripture, is full of meaning.

When I praise God, I am praising *what He is* in relation to me, and what He has done for me. He is my God. He is my Father. He is my Savior. He is my Creator. He is my Protector. He is my _____.

His Name

When I am led to "praise the name of Elohim, or bless His name, or trust in His name," keep in mind that *His name is who He is*. It represents all that He is, His character, His nature, His personality, His disposition, His temperament, His essence, His identity. His name is I AM. I AM holy. I AM faithful. I AM gracious. I AM merciful. I AM truth. I AM righteousness. I AM sovereign. I AM just. I AM love. I AM Who I AM.

When Vicki and I eat in a restaurant, I like to ask my server his or her name. Let's say it's Paul. I call him by his first name, and I say this: "Paul, we are about to pray. Is there something we can pray about for you?" I never fail to get an awkward smile, and a pretty good prayer request. I find that people value the act of calling them by name and asking how I can serve them. It makes an immediate connection.

So, God has a particular name: YHWH or Yahweh. I want to acknowledge His name in worship. I realize and understand that this name represents who He is. Next, I want to take my worship a step further personally; *I want to acknowledge what and who He is to me*.

Who is God to me? To worship Him, I must know Him, His nature, and His character, I can only know God as He chooses to reveal Himself. Throughout scripture, God has revealed Himself in many ways to many different people. In these revelations, these recipients have given God additional names of their own, special names that speak of His nature as He worked in their lives. We will study these special names and learn how and when to use them in our worship.

Today, when one dude greets another dude, he might say, "Hey Man, howzitgoin?" The greeted dude has a name, but the greeter just calls him "Man." It's not wrong, but he can do better. Out of respect, he can learn his name and use it. It makes an immediate connection. Calling YHWH "God" is a little like that. We can do better.

So far in this book I have referred to Yahweh as "God." I will likely continue to do so from time to time because, I suppose, it's become our familiar practice to call our Creator by His *title* rather than His true covenant name. But hence forth, I hope you will indulge my true desire to refer to Him, with the greatest respect and reverence, as Yahweh, Abba, Father, Lord, and God. I may even use the tetragrammaton from time to time just to emphasize the superiority and holiness of this name above all names.

7

NAMES OF GOD

"And those who know Your name will put their trust in You, For You, O LORD, have not forsaken those who seek You." (Psalm 9:10, NASB95)

What is the primary purpose for man's existence?

For what purpose were we created? Well, Genesis 1 says that God made man to rule over the creatures of the earth. His first command was to "be fruitful and multiply and subdue the earth." Is that why He made us? Genesis also says He made us in His own image. What does that mean? Do we look like God? In what ways are we like God? Why, after creating all this beauty and bounty, would God make us anything like Himself? And does the creation around us reflect God in some way? These are all good questions.[18]

> *Worship is what we were created for. This is the final end of all existence – the worship of God.*
>
> *God created the universe so that it would display the worth of His glory. And He created us so that we would see this glory and reflect it by knowing and loving it –with all our heart and soul and mind and strength.*
>
> —JOHN PIPER

I believe God made this magnificent universe and had no one to appreciate it but Himself. I think He wanted to share it with someone else who could appreciate all this beauty and be able to acknowledge Him as its creator. To agree with Him that "It was good." God did not create us because He was lonely or needed a gardener or zookeeper. He existed throughout all eternity past before He ever spoke our world into being. He had perfect fellowship and harmony within the Trinity long before planet earth came along. He did not really need us. (Of course, all these are just my personal notions. If yours are different, that's fine.)

One of the greatest statements ever written of our Christian faith is the Westminster Catechism, which completely declares the foundations and beliefs of Christianity. It begins with a question: "What is the chief and highest end of man?", then answers its own question. "Man's chief and highest end is to glorify God and fully enjoy Him forever."

In Isaiah 43 God speaks of all His people as those "whom I created for My glory." We were created for God's glory – not our own. Created to acknowledge God's glory and reflect God's glory. Paul told the Corinthians to "do all to the glory of God." (1 Cor. 10:31, NASB95)

The fact that God made us just for His own glory guarantees we have significance and worth. We were created to bring glory and honor to God and find joy in His presence. To "fellowship with Him forever." David the psalmist wrote songs about this chief aspect of life. He said, "In your presence there is the fullness of joy, in your right hand are pleasures forever." (Psalm 16:11, NASB95). Other psalmists wrote these words:

> "Whom have I in heaven but You? And besides You, I desire nothing on earth. My flesh and my heart may fail, But God is the strength of my heart and my portion forever." (Psalm 73:25–26, NASB95)

> "How lovely are Your dwelling places, O LORD of hosts! My soul longed and even yearned for the courts of the LORD; My heart and my flesh sing for joy to the living God." (Psalm 84:1–2, NASB95)

The fullness of joy can only be found in delighting yourself in the Lord and in the knowledge of His character. We were made to worship God.

We can worship Him only to the extent that we know Him.

Let me repeat that.

We can worship Him only to the extent that we know Him.

The prophet Hosea said, "for the lack of knowledge of God His people had been destroyed." (Author's translation)

Our task in chapter 7 will be solely this mission: discover the character and nature of the one true God to the extent possible in this limited forum. And, as a result, we should be able to acknowledge Him more fully and appropriately, bring glory to Him, and find joy for ourselves in His fellowship. If that seems like a lot, it is! God is way bigger than we can even imagine or ever write down in a book or in our hearts. In fact, the Bible itself is not sufficient to fully encompass the greatness and glory that is our Elohim. But let's try anyway.

Our method will be to learn some names given to God. Almost all these names come from stories in scripture where God revealed Himself to someone in a personal way that inspired him or her to apply a new descriptor to Him. A new designation for God that attributed a specific quality or character trait.

The Bible instructs us many times to "Glorify His Name."[19] Maybe the best way to do this is to *know* His name and recognize in Him the qualities His name proclaims. This knowledge will require us to learn a little more Hebrew. I've tried to make these names easy to pronounce, so give it a try. If you prefer, you can just use the English versions. Let's learn some of the names of God and acknowledge these wonderful attributes in Him. [20]

"God, You are_____"

He is Elohim

Pronunciation: el-ō-heem′

As you might expect, the very first sentence in the Bible contains the name of God. "In the beginning, *God* created the heavens and the earth."

The Hebrew word from which this word "God" is translated is the word *"ELOHIM"* (el-o-heem′ with emphasis on the last syllable). The Hebrew word *"ELOHIM"* is found 2570 times in scripture and is always translated into English as "God" or "gods" when it references "other gods." *ELOHIM* is derived from two Hebrew words. The first is *EL* which means mighty, prominent, and strong. *EL* appears 217 times in scripture and is also translated "God."

> "For the Lord (*YHWH*) your God (*ELOHIM*) is the God (*ELOHIM*) of gods (*ELOHIM*) and the Lord (*ADONAI*) of lords (*ADON*), the great, the mighty, and the awesome God (*EL*)…" (Deuteronomy 10:17a, NASB95 Author's translation added)

We see Elohim throughout the creation story. We see His great creative and governing power. We see His omnipotence and sovereignty.

The other word that Elohim is derived from is the word *"ALAH."* This word means to "declare or swear." Elohim makes a covenant with Abram: "By Myself I have sworn because there is none greater than Myself to swear by." (Genesis 22:16, NASB95)

It is Elohim who covenants with Noah, Abraham, and Moses. To Israel He says over and over again, "I will be your Elohim and you will be my people," (e.g., Jeremiah 30:22).

In the name "Elohim" we see a great God of creation and power, as well as a gentle God of relationship and fellowship.

> "In the beginning *ELOHIM* created (*BARA*) the heavens and the earth. The earth was formless and void, and darkness was over the surface of the deep, and the Spirit of *ELOHIM* was moving over the surface of the waters." (Genesis 1:1–2, NASB95 Author's translation added)

The word we translate as "Spirit" is *"RUACH."* It means "breath."

"The Breath of Elohim" at creation.

"In the beginning was the Word, and the Word was with God, and the Word was God. He was in the beginning with God. All things came into being through Him, and apart from Him nothing came into being that has come into being." (John 1:1–3, NASB95)

Here we see God the Son, the second person of the Trinity, participating in and sustaining creation. We see Him represented as the spoken Word of God, sent forth to accomplish creation. Consider how your words "go forth" from you to accomplish a task.

"And the Word became flesh, and dwelt among us, and we saw His glory, glory as of the only begotten from the Father, full of grace and truth." (John 1:14, NASB95)

Again, we see the Word of God sent forth to live among us, to represent, and reflect the glory of the Father.

"The Word of Elohim" at creation.

So, what do we know about Elohim now that we might not have known or realized before?

- Elohim is great and powerful and creative.
- Elohim seeks to have a personal relationship with us. A covenant of love.
- Elohim is a plurality of personalities and characteristics.
- He is Elohim the I AM, Father.
- He is The Breath of Elohim, Spirit.
- He is the Word of Elohim, Son.

> *Worship is simply giving God His breath back.*
>
> – LOUIE GIGLIO

I AM your God.

He is El Shaddai
Pronunciation: el shad-dah'ee

El, as we have learned, means "mighty, powerful, and prominent." El itself is translated as "God," particularly in circumstances that indicate the great power of God.

There is some debate among Hebrew scholars as to the derivation and meaning of this Hebrew word "*SHADDAI* (or *SHADDAY*)." It is most often translated as "Almighty." El Shaddai is translated as "Almighty God" or "God Almighty." It is easy for us to see God as being almighty and all powerful. Other scholars propose that *SHADDAI* derives from the Hebrew word *SHAD*, or breast (*SHADAYIM* – breasts).

So, which is it? Maybe both.

Isaiah 66:12–13 gives us a clear picture of the meaning of this name, although the name isn't used here. In these verses, God is speaking about the people of Jerusalem.

> "For thus says the LORD, 'Behold, I extend <u>peace</u> to her like a <u>river</u>, And the glory of the nations like an <u>overflowing</u> stream; And you will be <u>nursed</u>, you will be <u>carried</u> on the hip and <u>fondled</u> on the knees. As one whom his <u>mother comforts</u>, so I will <u>comfort</u> you; And you will be <u>comforted</u> in Jerusalem.'" (Isaiah 66:12–13, NASB95)

Women who've nursed or breastfed babies can clearly understand the picture God is giving us in these verses. When a baby is hungry, nursing at his mother's breast will fill and satisfy. When a baby is crying, the breast will comfort and soothe. The breast both nourishes and satisfies.

The concept of a breasted god was well-known to the ancients. Isis was an Egyptian goddess clustered over with breasts. Diana, the Ephesian/Greek goddess, was also depicted with many breasts.

The picture of El Shaddai is this: one mighty and capable to nourish, satisfy, and supply. The one who pours out blessing. The source of blessing, fullness, and fruitfulness. The all-sufficient, all-bountiful one.

While the meaning of this name seems simple and clear, I believe only a special few Christians ever really know and experience God by this wonderful name. Let me explain.

As *Elohim*, God was known as creator of the world. Of all mankind.

As *Yahweh*, God was known as the great "I Am" to a special group of people from among all mankind, the nation Israel.

But, as *El Shaddai*, God reveals Himself only 48 times in the Bible, often in special circumstances and dealings with select individuals from within his people Israel. As I have studied this name, *I have come to believe that only a few of God's children ever know Him as El Shaddai.*

While God wants to be known by all of us as El Shaddai, blesser, filler, the all-sufficient one, I think El Shaddai is the most intimate of God's names. What's more intimate than a babe at its mother's breast?

Unfortunately, many of us – by our own choices and actions – resist and circumvent God and His work in our lives. We don't allow Him to become our All-Sufficient El Shaddai, able to supply every need we have.

God's Word shows us what is required of us to know Him as El Shaddai. We see in scripture three things we must do if we're to know God, intimately, as El Shaddai:

1. *We must allow God to change us, not just save us.*

Abraham, A man willing to be changed by God (Gen. 17:1–6)

> "Now when Abram was ninety-nine years old, the LORD appeared to Abram and said to him, 'I am God Almighty (El Shaddai); Walk before Me and be blameless (complete).'" (Genesis 17:1, NASB95 Author's translation added)

This is the first time the name El Shaddai, God Almighty, is used in scripture.

> "Abram fell on his face, and God talked with him, saying, 'As for Me, behold, My covenant is with you, And you will be the father of a multitude of nations. No longer shall your name be called Abram, But your name shall be Abraham; For I will make you the father of a multitude of nations.'" (Genesis 17:3–5, NASB95)

Remember, Abram meant "*exalted* father."

But God didn't want Abram to be exalted because of his vast flocks, his riches, and his reputation among men. These gifts could be viewed as Abram's own doing. Instead, God wanted to make Abram fruitful for Him; He began this by changing his name to Abraham, which means "father of a multitude." This change could only be done by God Himself. Abram was nearly 100 years old and was "as good as dead," Romans 4:19 (NASB95) tells us. Perhaps one reason Abram was chosen for this daunting task was because He *was* so old, and only El Shaddai could get the glory.

> "I have made you exceedingly fruitful, and I will make nations of you, and kings will come forth from you." (Genesis 17:6, NASB95)

When God revealed Himself to Abram as El Shaddai, Abram had to let God change his nature from one of self-sufficiency and self-effort (Ishmael's father) to one of God-sufficiency and God-dependency (Isaac's father).

Abram had to be "as dead," in *his flesh*, for God to put His own nature into him. God put into Abram's name the chief letter of His own name Yahweh. The Hebrew letter "He." The "ha" sound.

For God to do this, Abraham had to recognize his own insufficiency. He had to acknowledge that nothing good or fruitful could come from himself, but that all the blessings and riches of life were from El Shaddai alone.

We must yield and surrender to God to know Him as El Shaddai.

2. *We must allow God to afflict us, not just bless us.*

Jacob and Job, Men willing to be afflicted by God (Gen. 32 and 35; Job 5, 40 and 42).

Like Abraham and Sarah, Jacob was a man who persevered with God in order that God could change his name and his nature. And, like Abraham and Sarah, the change in Jacob's life came with difficulty and affliction.

> "Then Jacob was left alone, and a man wrestled with him until daybreak. When he saw that he had not prevailed against him, he touched the socket of his thigh; so the socket of <u>Jacob's thigh was dislocated while he wrestled with him</u>." (Genesis 32:24–25, NASB95)

> "God said to him, 'Your name is Jacob; You shall no longer be called Jacob (to follow), But Israel (to contend or fight) shall be your name.' Thus He called him Israel. God also said to him, '<u>I am God Almighty</u>; Be fruitful and multiply; A nation and a company of nations shall come from you, And kings shall come forth from you.'" (Genesis 35:10–11, NASB95 Author's translation added)

Jacob came to know God as El Shaddai only after God afflicted him and dislocated his hip. Many of us are like Jacob; we contend with God and resist His leading. The only way He can get us to hear Him is with affliction of some sort, perhaps to the degree that it takes to get our attention. God is truly gracious, but He means business.

Then there is Job. We all know the story of Job. God gave Satan permission to kill Job's flocks and servants by fire and enemy attack, then destroy his children and house by a great wind, presumably a tornado or hurricane. God brought Job to that incredible place in his spiritual journey where Job said,

> "Naked I came from my mother's womb, and naked I shall return there. The Lord gave, and the Lord has taken away. Blessed be the name of the Lord." (Job 1:21, NASB95)

Job understood his own insufficiency and dependence on God.

It's significant that of the 48 uses of El Shaddai in the Old Testament, 31 are in the book of Job.

> "Behold, how happy is the man whom God reproves, So do not despise the discipline of the Almighty. For He inflicts pain, and gives relief; He wounds, and His hands also heal." (Job 5:17–18, NASB95)

Job's life teaches us that the greatest blessings of God often come through adversity and difficulty. For only in them will we learn that God's grace, strength, and power are sufficient for every need. And *only* if we accept and embrace afflictions and difficulties – and receive them as blessings from God – can we know Him and see Him by His wonderful name, El Shaddai.

When affliction comes, ask God to reveal Himself as El Shaddai.

3. *We must allow God to empty us so He can fill us.*

Paul, A man willing to be emptied by God (Phil. 4:12–13).

Like Abraham and Jacob, Paul was a man who had his name and nature changed by God. The Lord touched Saul, the persecutor of Christians, in a heavenly light on the road to Damascus; dramatically converted, Saul was changed into Paul, a man filled with the Holy Spirit. Paul was perhaps the most fruitful Christian who ever lived.

One of the most significant things about Paul's walk with Christ was how he learned to be empty. In Philippians 4 Paul said this:

> "I know how to get along with humble means, and I also know how to live in prosperity; in any and every circumstance <u>I have learned the secret of being filled</u> and going hungry, both of having abundance and suffering need. I can do all things through Him who strengthens me. Nevertheless, you have done well to share with me in my affliction." (Philippians 4:12–14, NASB95)

What *was* Paul's secret of being filled in Phil. 4:12?

I believe it was in being completely dependent on the filler, El Shaddai, at whose breast he nursed as a little child, moment by moment, day by day. The God whose life flowed into and out of Him, in fruitfulness and service.

In both his times of plenty and his times of want, in times of victory and times of defeat, Paul was connected to his El Shaddai. He learned that the more "full of self" he was, the less blessing God could pour into him. Paul remained connected to Him as the branch abides in the vine. Jesus said:

> "I am the vine, you are the branches; he who abides in Me and I in him, he bears much fruit, for apart from Me you can do nothing." (John 15:5, NASB95)

Because he depended totally on God, Paul had the joy, peace, and spiritual blessing that comes only from intimacy with El Shaddai.

Paul was also familiar with God-imposed affliction.

> "Because of the surpassing greatness of the revelations, for this reason, to keep me from exalting myself, there was given me a thorn in the flesh, a messenger of Satan to torment me—to keep me from exalting myself! Concerning this I implored the Lord three times that it might leave me. And He has said to me, 'My grace is sufficient for you, for power is perfected in weakness.' Most gladly, therefore, I will rather boast about my weaknesses, so that the power of Christ may dwell in me. Therefore, I am well content with weaknesses, with insults, with distresses, with persecutions, with difficulties, for Christ's sake; for when I am weak, then I am strong." (2 Corinthians 12:7–10, NASB95)

Paul knew the fullness and fruitfulness of his El Shaddai.

We must first be emptied if we will ever be filled by El Shaddai.

Only those of us willing to be changed by God, afflicted by Him, and emptied by Him will ever know the sufficiency, fullness, blessing, and intimacy of El Shaddai. When we yield to Him, we will find in Him, and Him alone, all we need for a satisfied life.

> "Abraham breathed his last and died in a ripe old age, an old man and satisfied with life ..." (Genesis 25:8a, NASB95)

I AM your Might.
I AM your Sufficiency.

He is El Roi

Pronunciation: el ro-ee′ (seeing)
Alternate: El Raah - rah-aah′ (sees)

The story of Abram/Abraham and Sarai/Sarah is a fascinating one. God promised to make Abram the father of a nation, but to do this He had to produce a child. Abram and Sarai were both in their 90s when this promise was given to them, before God changed their names.

> "Now Sarai, Abram's wife had borne him no children, and she had an Egyptian maid whose name was Hagar. So Sarai said to Abram, 'Now behold, the LORD has prevented me from bearing children. Please go in to my maid; perhaps I will obtain children through her.' And Abram listened to the voice of Sarai." (Genesis 16:1–2, NASB95)

God expected Abram to have faith in Him. Faith often requires patience. But, like many of us, Abram got impatient with God and took matters into his own hands; Sarai's maid Hagar soon became pregnant. As you might expect, this situation caused some tension between the two women. Sarai mistreated Hagar and she fled.

> "Now the angel of the LORD found her by a spring of water in the wilderness, by the spring on the way to Shur. He said, 'Hagar, Sarai's maid, where have you come from and where are you going?' And she said, 'I am fleeing from the presence of my mistress Sarai.' Then the angel of the LORD said to her, 'Return to your mistress, and submit yourself to her authority.' Moreover, the angel of the LORD said to her, 'I will greatly multiply your descendants so that they will be too many to count.' The angel of the LORD said to her further, 'Behold, you are with child, and you will bear a son; and you shall call his name Ishmael …

> And he will live to the east of all his brothers.'" (Genesis 16:7–11a, 12b, NASB95)

You might think because of Abram's disobedience, God would not bless Hagar or her child. But this conundrum was not her fault. An "angel of YHWH" came to encourage her, which was a common way that YHWH Himself might approach a person (perhaps so the person would not be frightened). The Hebrew word we translate "angel" is "*MALAK.*" It simply means "messenger." "*ANGLOS*" is the Greek word for "messenger" and "angel" in the New Testament. Abraham would later encounter this same "messenger" as would Jacob, Gideon, and many others. In all cases, before the encounter was over YHWH had revealed Himself as the one bringing the message. Hagar recognized the "Angel" for who He really was. She understood His message and received God's blessing.

> "Then she called the name of *YHWH* (the LORD) who spoke to her, 'You are a God who sees'; for she said, 'Have I even remained alive here after seeing Him?'" (Genesis 16:7–13, NASB95 Author's translation added)

At times God may seem far away. He may be quiet for a time to test your faith or your obedience. Keep this truth in mind: if God seems far away it was you who moved. He is always present. Near. Within. Always.

Hagar recognized that God not only "saw" her but understood her dilemma. He reassured her that everything would turn out all right, and her son Ishmael would have many descendants. As God promised, Ishmael would indeed have many descendants. His offspring would become the Arab peoples who then (and now) "live to the east of his brothers." Hagar, a handmaid, a servant, would come to give God this wonderful name and help us realize that God, our El, sees us and understands our situation far better than we do. No matter how far we have drifted or run away, He is there to reassure us and get us back on track.

I AM the El who sees you.

I see you.

He is Adonai
Pronunciation: ad-ō-nī′

In our effort to come to know God better we have studied "Elohim." We found Elohim to be the pre-existent, never-changing God of creation. We saw the "breath of Elohim" in the creation story, the Holy Spirit. We also saw the "Word of Elohim" in creation, the catalyst of creation, the Son of God, Jesus.

We have seen Elohim as the great and powerful God of Creation but also as Yahweh, the gentle and loving God of Covenant. Yahweh desires to have a love relationship with each of us; but this is *His* covenant, not ours.

I worked many years in the information technology supply chain. We have a phrase in business when we are negotiating a contract with a vendor. Before we sign a contract, we want to know, "What are the Ts and Cs?" We want to know the Terms and Conditions of the contract. It's true that God desires to have a close relationship with each of us. But before we can enter into this covenant relationship, we must know the Ts and Cs. In God's contract, He holds all the cards. He gets to decide all the Ts and Cs. We get to decide whether we accept them and sign the contract, or whether we don't and refuse to sign. This relationship is our choice. If we want to enter into this covenant with Yahweh, we do so on His terms.

But here is the big rub with most Americans: we want to negotiate with God. We want Him to concede on this point or that. We want the freedom to explore all our options, but still reap the benefits of believing in God. We want to do some good works and earn some points we can spend later. *We want to live our own lives and get to call on Him when we need Him and go to heaven when we die.*

Recently there was a poll of Americans about their (so-called) "religious beliefs." (You usually read these polls in the paper on Easter Sunday.) This poll said that more than 90% of the people in America say they believe in God. Really!? Ninety percent?

It's actually kind of easy to believe in a God of creation. I mean look around. Here it is! It's much easier to believe this world was created than to believe it all just evolved from the slime. A newborn baby is just too remarkable for any other explanation. We *want* to believe in a God who is powerful and great. One who is the creator. One who sustains life. A God who is on our side. That's all so comforting and safe. No wonder 90% percent of Americans "believe" in God. We need to feel "comforted and safe" in a world that changes so rapidly.

During the American Civil War, both sides were absolutely convinced *they* were doing the will of God and that He was on *their* side. It's become easy, especially here in the southern U.S., just to check the box and join a church; then when it comes up in conversation, you have an acceptable answer for your belief in God. "O sure, we go to Third Pres." (Or wherever.)

God has revealed Himself as Yahweh and Elohim, the God of covenant and creation. He requires us to respond to Him in ways that reflect our attitude toward such a God. He made us in His image, so He holds us accountable to *be* like Him. Paul said:

> "and put on the new self, which in the likeness of God has been created in righteousness and holiness of the truth." (Ephesians 4:24, NASB95)

To "put on a new self" implies we must lay aside the "old self." To be in right relationship with God we must believe He exists *and submit our ways to His ways.* We must truly believe Jesus died and came back to life. We must deny ourselves and take up *His* cross and follow, not lead or resist. These requirements are some of the Ts and Cs of the New Covenant.

We learn a word from scripture that exemplifies this relationship. This word speaks volumes about a right relationship between God and us. It defines our relationship to Elohim. It is the simple word "Lord."

Over 400 times in the Old Testament "Lord" is used as a name for God, not counting the thousands of times it's spelled LORD in all caps. When you see the word "Lord" as a name for God, it is the Hebrew word "*ADONAI*." It denotes master or ruler (not overbearing possessor or owner, not equal partner, nor companion). It speaks of a benevolent master/ servant relationship. The name "Adonai" signifies God's position as the one in charge and suggests who God is in relation to us.

"Lord" also suggests who we are in relation to God! It was Adonai who called Abram, Moses, Gideon, and David into action. Like Elohim, Adonai is always used in the plural form as a matter of respect and amplification, as a name for God.

(*ADON* or *ADONI* = lord or master – *ADONAI* or *ADONAY* = my Lords)

In Malachi *ADON* is used twice where God compares Himself to a human master:

> "A son honors his father, and a servant his master (*ADON*). 'Then if I am a father, where is My honor? And if I am a master (*ADON*), where is My respect?' says the LORD of hosts to you," (Malachi 1:6a, NASB95 Author's translation added)

Let's look at some examples of the three names of God that we've learned so far. Listen to how they are used. Listen to the context. Notice how they are used together in the same sentence. Notice the word "name" and how it's used. As you read these examples, replace our English word with the Hebrew name for God. When you see YHWH, pronounce it as "Yahweh."

"O *YHWH* (Lord,) our *ADONAI* (Lord,) how majestic is Your <u>name</u> in all the earth, who have displayed Your splendor above the heavens!" (Psalm 8:1, NASB95 Author's translation added)

"Preserve me, O *ELOHIM* (God,) for I take refuge in You. I said to *YHWH* (the Lord), 'You are my *ADONAI* (Lord;) I have no good besides You.'" (Psalm 16:1–2, NASB95 Author's translation added)

"To You, O *YHWH* (Lord,) I called, and to the *ADONAI* (Lord) I made supplication:" (Psalm 30:8, NASB95 Author's translation added)

"Let all who seek You rejoice and be glad in You; Let those who love Your salvation say continually, '*YHWH* (The Lord) be magnified!' Since I am afflicted and needy, Let the *ADONAI* (Lord) be mindful of me. You are my help and my deliverer; Do not delay, O my *ELOHIM* (God.)" (Psalm 40:16–17, NASB95 Author's translation added)

"Behold, *ELOHIM* (God) is my helper; *ADONAI* (The Lord) is the sustainer of my soul." (Psalm 54:4, NASB95 Author's translation added)

The people of Israel had no problem understanding this relationship of Lord and servant. They lived as slaves to one master or another for centuries. Strict rules governed this relationship. They understood that the master or "*ADONI*" (singular) had the right to expect complete and unquestioned obedience. Lordship meant complete submission by the servant. But this relationship was not one-sided. The master was responsible to protect and provide for the needs of his slaves. And, so it is with our relationship with "Adonai." God created us to respect and obey Him as Lord but, in return for our complete submission to Him as Lord, He promises to protect us and provide for our needs. A master never required a slave to perform a task unless he first provided the abilities and tools with which to accomplish his will. He provided shelter and food for the well-being of his servants. However, if a slave rebelled against the master, he was punished and fell outside the master's protecting hand.

We can easily see how this master/slave relationship of ancient times closely parallels our own relationship with Adonai, The Lord our Elohim.

One more thing about that master/slave relationship of old: a Hebrew master could keep a slave for only seven years. After the seventh year, the slave could decide to leave the master and fend for himself as a free man. Or, if he chose, he could remain with the master as his slave for life. If the slave loved the master enough to stay, he would go to the doorpost of the master's house, place his ear lobe against the wooden frame, and someone would pierce his ear with a pointed tool like an awl.

Then they would place a special earring in the slave's ear, and this ring would mark the slave as a slave for life.

Glad, one of the pioneer bands of contemporary Christian music, sang a great song along this same theme.

> Pierce my ear oh Lord my God.
> Take me to your door this day.
> I will serve no other God.
> Lord I'm here to stay.
> For you have paid the price for me.
> With your blood you've ransomed me.
> I will serve you eternally.
> A free man I'll never be.[35]

We have these same choices: to rebel or relent. Escape or submit. Ignore or obey. To be a part-time servant or a lifetime slave.

Some people say that Jesus must be Lord *of all*, or He is not lord *at all*. I'm not sure how true that really is. One thing I know is true: it *is* easy just to believe in Elohim and take our relationship with Him as a casual part of life. To want a part-time relationship with God that allows us to hang on to our sin and live like we want. Many Christians prefer this half-hearted relationship to God. I know it's true because we see these kinds of relationship so often, even among "church people." I see this "have-it-my-way" Christianity in my own church. If not careful, we can see it in ourselves.

Granted, it is not easy to commit yourself fully to God as Adonai. To make Him Lord of every aspect of your life. To submit to Him and His will and His requirements. It is not easy to trust Him for your protection and provision when the world says, "Come on man, *get* all you can, *while* you can." I also know that *this* is true: the only way ever to find and experience real joy in life is to worship Elohim as creator... and submit to Adonai as master and provider.

I AM your Lord.

He is Abba

Pronunciation: ah'-bah

So much of our concept of God arises from the image of the great and mighty God of creation. When we think of the God of the Bible, He is high and lifted up, terrible, frightening, and not to be trifled with. The great and powerful Oz, behind the curtain, moving the levers of mankind.

> *Worship is God's enjoyment of us and our enjoyment of him. Worship is a response to the father/child relationship.*
>
> – GRAHAM KENDRICK

"Say unto God, How terrible art thou in thy works! Through the greatness of thy power shall thine enemies submit themselves unto thee." (Psalm 66:3, KJV)

He sounds all the more frightening in this language of King James!

True, God is high and lifted up. He is the God of creation. But our God is a dichotomy of personalities, great and mighty on one hand and loving and tender on the other. This contrast is perhaps why so many people have difficulty understanding our God.

We often transfer the personality of our own earthly father onto God. If our father was mean and strict, then God becomes the same. Or, if our father was absent, then so is God.

If we do this, we may find it more difficult to understand God as a kind and loving father. How can God be both absolutely just and absolutely loving? Earthly fathers are usually more one than the other, but our God is perfectly both.

We definitely worship God for His power, magnificence, and glory. He is all these things. But we may also worship Him as our loving father and tender caregiver.

I've spoken before about my daddy. That's what all his kids called him – "Daddy." But there were times when he was "father," the head of the house who was willing to dole out the "whippins" when necessary.

Believe me, God will assume this role of disciplinarian, if needed. But mostly my daddy was just "Daddy." But how can God be "Daddy?"

"*ABBA*" is the Aramaic word used as a familiar term for father. "Ab" means father, but "Abba" was derived from "baby-talk." Think of "da-da" that a baby might say as she is learning to say "Daddy." Eventually people broadened the use of Abba to include any father. This word appears only three times in the New Testament. The time that really gets to me is found in the gospel of Mark when Jesus is in the middle of His impassioned prayer to His Father.

"And He went a little beyond them and fell to the ground and began to pray that if it were possible, the hour might pass Him by. And He was saying, 'Abba! Father! All things are possible for You; remove this cup from Me; yet not what I will, but what You will.'" (Mark 14:35–36, NASB95)

I never really appreciated the impact of this name for God until I was on a long flight to Israel several years ago. I sat behind a young Israeli family whom I assumed was traveling back home from America. There was the mom and the dad, and between them two small children. The little boy, maybe six or seven, would call out to his father as "Abba." He wanted to sit in Abba's lap. They spoke modern Hebrew, but it was clear that "Abba" was his daddy.

"If you then, being evil, know how to give good gifts to your children, how much more will your Father who is in heaven give what is good to those who ask Him!" (Matthew 7:11, NASB95)

Abba is the God who gives good gifts to His children. But exactly how is it that we are His children? Doesn't culture say that we are <u>all</u> God's children?

"For all who are being led by the Spirit of God, these are sons of God. For you have not received a spirit of slavery leading to fear again, but you have received a spirit of adoption as sons by which we cry out, 'Abba! Father!' The Spirit Himself testifies with our spirit that we are children of God, and if children, heirs also, heirs of God and fellow heirs with Christ, if indeed we suffer with Him so that we may also be glorified with Him." (Romans 8:14–17, NASB95)

All born-again believers and followers of Christ have living *within us* His Holy Spirit. In the same way that YHWH "dwelt" in the temples of stone, Holy Spirit dwells in our temples of flesh. (Maybe not exactly the same way, but similar.) Holy Spirit "testifies" with our spirit and "tells us the truth" about our adoption by God as His own child. God chose us and brought us into His family. I have a nephew and niece who were chosen and adopted by my older brother and sister-in-law. They are as much a part of our large family as are my own biological children. If God sees us as His own children, then we can see Him as Abba, Daddy.

There will be times in your worship when you will want to address God as YHWH, Adonai, or El Shaddai, names that reflect His might, grandeur, and lordship. But there will also be times when He is just "Daddy." Your personal, tender, and loving Abba. So, climb up in His lap and enjoy His love.

I AM your loving Father.

He is Yahweh

Pronunciation: yah'-way

Alternate: yah-vey or yeh-ho'-vah or Jah-ho'-vah

Note: When you see YHWH, pronounce it with the vowels, Yahweh.

In chapter 6, we ran across Moses listening to God speak from a burning bush. Moses asked God to identify Himself so he would know just whom he was to represent. How did God reply? "I AM who I AM; tell them I AM has sent you." The Hebrew word for I AM is this word "*YHWH*," His covenant name. It is with YHWH that we have our agreement or covenant. (He is our God and we serve Him alone.) As I said before, I have discovered that God's very nature, as well as His relationship to us, can be found in studying His names. God has many names attributed to Himself. But why would God have so many names in Scripture? Because no one name could be adequate to describe His greatness. If David was known as shepherd, giant-killer, king of Israel, writer, poet, and musician, then certainly an infinite God who is King of Kings and Lord of Lords must be known by many different names. God is too multi-faceted and powerful to be contained in just one name. He has revealed these different aspects of His character so we can get to know Him more completely.

I AM.

GREG DIXON

He is Yahweh-Rophe

Pronunciation: yah'-way – ro-phay'
Alternate: yah'-way – rah-fah'

The Hebrew words "*ROPHE*" or "*RAPHA*" mean to heal, restore to normal, or make whole again. They can also mean to save. These words are found 68 times in the Old Testament.

God first reveals Himself as Yahweh-Rophe in Exodus 15, right after His deliverance of the Israelites at the Red Sea.

> "Then Moses led Israel from the Red Sea, and they went out into the wilderness of Shur; and they went three days in the wilderness and found no water. When they came to Marah, they could not drink the waters of Marah, for they were bitter; therefore, it was named Marah. So, the people grumbled at Moses, saying, 'What shall we drink?' Then he cried out to the LORD, and the LORD showed him a tree; and he threw it into the waters, and the waters became sweet. There He made for them a statute and regulation, and there He tested them. And He said, 'If you will give earnest heed to the voice of the LORD your God, and do what is right in His sight, and give ear to His commandments, and keep all His statutes, I will put none of the diseases on you which I have put on the Egyptians; <u>for I, the LORD, am your healer.</u>'" (Exodus 15:22–26, NASB95)

Theologians tell us this "tree" symbolizes or pictures the cross of Christ, with the bitter waters representing the waters of sin and death. In salvation, which is our spiritual healing, we exchange the bitter waters of death with the rivers of living water that come from a relationship with Christ. Our spiritual healing comes from the tree (or cross) of Christ being cast into the bitter waters of our sinful lives.

In this Exodus passage, God tested the Israelites' faith in Him to provide (verse 25); He promised if they heeded His voice and did what was right in His sight that He would put none of the diseases on them that He put on the Egyptians. He said (verse 26), "For I, the LORD, am your Healer." Literally, God said, "*I, YHWH ROPHE.*" He established a key principle in the original covenant with His people: obedience brings blessing; disobedience brings judgment. This passage had specific application to the Israelites at that time, rather than to all men for all times. But what is God revealing about Himself here? First, what were the "diseases" He put on the Egyptians? Of the 10, the plague of boils was the only one that was anything like a disease (look it up). So, I see two ideas here: first, the Israelites were well aware of the plagues that broke the Pharaoh's will and gave them their escape from Egypt. They clearly understood what obedience would avoid. Second, "ROPHE" or "healer" must refer to things other than diseases. I am sure a real theologian would probably scoff at my rookie attempt at exegesis but let them.

> "Bless the LORD, O my soul, and forget none of His benefits; Who pardons all your iniquities, Who heals all your diseases;" (Psalm 103:2–3, NASB95)

All I know for sure is that God does not heal all my diseases, at least not here in my *earthly* being. So, since God is true to Himself, then His "healing" must apply to other things besides physical sickness. Also, Yahweh-Rophe (not me) decides if and how my healing might take place. The healing that Yahweh-Rophe speaks to in the Bible encompasses more than physical illnesses and diseases. Healing encompasses God's power to restore broken hearts, broken homes, broken dreams, broken relationships, broken childhoods, broken memories, as well as broken bodies. Suffering assumes many forms, but Christ's death on the cross for us releases a source of healing at every dimension of our need.

> "But He was pierced through for our transgressions, He was crushed for our iniquities; The chastening for our well-being fell upon Him, And by His scourging we are healed (RAPHA)." (Isaiah 53:5, NASB95 Author's translation added)

Yahweh-Rapha in the Old Testament is Yeshua Hamashiach in the New. Jesus the Messiah. Jesus healed many people in many ways. In fact, there's no record of His not healing someone who asked Him. He had compassion and healed their diseases, but physical healings and other miracles were incidental to His chief mission of saving and healing the souls of men and women. His miraculous healings proved His identity, His "God credentials." His primary invitation was more like, "Come to me, and I will give you rest for your souls."

After saying all that, after setting the stage for what theologians call a cessationist point of view, do I believe that God still heals our physical diseases? Yes, I do.

(Cessationism is the belief that spiritual gifts such as speaking in tongues, prophecy, and miraculous healing ceased with the Apostolic Age. Reformers such as John Calvin originated this view.)

Consider this thought: if God's people, those with gifts of healing, could heal really sick people at will, the way Jesus did, then we wouldn't need doctors or hospitals. People would line up at their "healing clinics" and state their "belief" in God, just to get their healing.

God would be nothing more than Santa Claus, and faith in God would become cheap, easy, and counterfeit.

So how does the gift of healing work today? First, how does it *not* work? There are charlatans who live wealthy lives selling prayer cloths and bottles of healing oil on TV. They stand on stages in big arenas and proclaim healings to whomever can qualify as healable and get past their bouncers. They heal a lot of hearing problems and one leg shorter than the other.

Jesus warned us of these in Matthew 7:15–23 (NASB95). He called them "ravenous wolves" and cast them out.

From my own observation, here's how it *does* work: there are the quiet, humble folk with a God-given gift, a simple message, and a *massive* faith. They believe that God loves us, and He can and will still heal our physical diseases. It takes some effort in prayer and a genuine desire to be healed. And, when He chooses, God still works miracles. He is (still) Yahweh-Rophe.

> "*YHWH* (The Lord) builds up Jerusalem; He gathers the outcasts of Israel.
> He heals (*RAPHA*) the brokenhearted and binds up their wounds." (Psalm
> 147:2–3, NASB95 Author's translation added)

I AM your Healer.

He is Yahweh-Nissi

Pronunciation: yah-way′ – nee′-see

Are you fighting any spiritual battles right now? In your family? In your witness? In your body? In your mind? In the world?

Well, we should be.

Maturing, serious-minded Christians *will* be in spiritual battle against the enemies of God and us, His children. Warfare is part of God's plan and purpose for us.

> "Fight the good fight of faith; take hold of the eternal life to which you were called, and you made the good confession in the presence of many witnesses." (1 Timothy 6:12, NASB95)

> "I have fought the good fight, I have finished the course, I have kept the faith; in the future there is laid up for me the crown of righteousness…" (2 Timothy 4:7–8, NASB95)

The name of God – Yahweh-Nissi – is revealed to us in spiritual battle. Look at its context in Exodus 17:8.

> "Then Amalek came and fought against Israel at Rephidim. So, Moses said to Joshua, 'Choose men for us and go out, fight against Amalek. Tomorrow I will station myself on the top of the hill <u>with the staff of God in my hand</u>.' Joshua did as Moses told him, and fought against Amalek; and Moses, Aaron, and Hur went up to the top of the hill. So it came about when Moses held his hand up (with the staff), that Israel prevailed, and when he let his hand down, Amalek prevailed. But Moses' hands were heavy. Then they took a stone and put it under him, and he sat on it; and Aaron and Hur supported his hands, one on one side and one on the other. Thus his hands were steady until the sun set. So Joshua overwhelmed Amalek and his people with the edge of the sword. Then YHWH (the Lord) said to Moses, 'Write this in a book as a memorial and recite it to Joshua, that I will utterly blot out the memory of Amalek from under heaven.'
>
> Moses built an altar and named it <u>The Lord is My Banner</u> (Yahweh-Nissi)." (Exodus 17:8–15, NASB95 Author's translation added)

Greg Dixon

The staff Moses held was perhaps his Midianite shepherd's staff that Yahweh turned into the staff of God (Ex. 4). As God's representative before Pharaoh, Moses released it to the ground, and it became a serpent. Then, when he picked it up, it was God's staff again. This same staff later turned the Nile River into blood (Exodus 7). It struck the dust of the ground which became gnats throughout Egypt (Exodus 8). BTW, I hate gnats! This staff sent thunder, hail, and fire down to the earth (Exodus 9). It directed an east wind that brought locusts on the land of Egypt (Exodus 10). The same staff divided the Red Sea for the Israelites so they could go through the midst of it on dry land (Exodus 14). In Exodus 17 it was Moses's "banner" in battle.

The staff, rod, or banner of God symbolized and pledged His presence, power, and working in battle. It represented God's own victorious identity. It was like wearing His team colors or going out to fight in His name. The purpose of the banner was to bring faith and confidence to God's people.

In ancient times, a banner was an insignia on a long pole, carried to give a group a rallying point. Banners often called an army to assemble or signaled that a battle was to begin. It gave an army its identity.

> "Now the LORD spoke to Moses and to Aaron, saying, 'The sons of Israel shall camp, each by his own standard, with the banners of their fathers' households; they shall camp around the tent of meeting at a distance.'" (Numbers 2:1–2, NASB95)

When I was a sophomore in high school, I was the guidon bearer for Company Bravo in Reserve Officers Training Corp, ROTC. Each day when we were called to order, the three platoons lined up in ranks. I stood right out in front and held a polished pole, with a brass point, about seven feet long. A yellow triangular flag on top simply bore the letter "B." My guidon signified where to form ranks. It also distinguished us from the Alpha, Charlie, Delta, and Echo companies when we were on parade on the football field. I was promoted to platoon leader as a junior and became the company commander of Bravo in my senior year. As a leader I always appreciated the importance of my company guidon and its bearer. I counted on him being in position with his guidon pointed to the sky.

The banner in Old Testament times was not necessarily a flag as we use nowadays. Think more of a big triangular banner, the pennant of your sports team. Often this banner was a bare pole with an ornament on the top, molded from bronze, that glittered and shone in the sun. Or the pole might have a carved figure of an animal, bird, or reptile. The word in Exodus 17:15 for banner is also translated in other O.T. verses as pole, ensign, or standard.

When Moses held up the banner in Exodus 17, the Israelites went forth victoriously in God's power and strength. When he let it down, they were defeated. But remember? The rod in Moses's hand was only a symbol. It represented the victory God had provided and demonstrated His vital role in the battles of His people. Also keep in mind that the ones fighting in Exodus 17 were really Joshua and his warriors, not Moses. Moses was an old man who indirectly participated in the battle – as an encourager – with his two friends, all situated on the hill overlooking the battlefield in an attitude of prayer. But Moses recognized the power of Yahweh-Nissi as the rallying point. Like the Israelites in battle then, we belong to God and are of His army. We fight our battles under His banner, raised high. We know He has already won the victory over Satan and the world. And, in Him, our victory is assured.

One more banner story.

"So the people came to Moses and said, 'We have sinned, because we have spoken against the LORD and you; intercede with the LORD, that He may remove the serpents from us.' And Moses interceded for the people. Then the LORD said to Moses, 'Make a fiery serpent, and set it on a standard (*NISSI*); and it shall come about, that everyone who is bitten, when he looks at it, he will live.' And Moses made a bronze serpent and set it on the standard (*NISSI*); and it came about, that if a serpent bit any man, when he looked to the bronze serpent, he lived." (Numbers 21:7–9, NASB95 Author's translation added)

"As Moses lifted up the serpent in the wilderness, even so must the Son of Man be lifted up; so that whoever believes will in Him have eternal life." (John 3:14–15, NASB95)

"And I, if I am lifted up from the earth, will draw all men to Myself." (John 12:32, NASB95)

Of course, the "*NISSI*" is a picture (or type) of the cross, and Jesus is the banner upon it. As we worship Him, we might be reminded of the time He spent there on the cross, suspended between heaven and earth. He became our rallying point, our standard, our victory over sin and death. But praise God! He is no longer there, but rather sitting triumphantly before us, kingly in appearance, still being our banner. Still leading us in victory.

What spiritual battles are you fighting within yourself or in the world? What's your strategy for victory? Are you going in your own strength and power? Or are you under God's banner, wearing His armor, standing on His Word, fervent in prayer, strong in worship?

"What then shall we say to these things? If God is for us, who is against us? He who did not spare His own Son, but delivered Him over for us all, how will He not also with Him freely give us all things?

"But in all these things we overwhelmingly conquer through Him who loved us." (Romans 8:31–32, 37, NASB95)

I Am your Banner.

He is Yahweh-M'Kaddesh

Pronunciation: yah-way′ – ma-kā′-desh

Yahweh revealed Himself to Moses as the God of righteousness and holiness. In turn, God requires these same righteous traits of us. But we get hung up on holiness; we think of it as perfection and without fault. There is no doubt that YHWH is perfect and without fault. That is an absolute, and only He meets the requirement absolutely.

The root word from which M'Kaddesh is derived is "*QÂDOSH*" or "*KADŌSH*." It means sacred or holy. Other associated words – "*QŌDESH*" or "*KŌDESH*" and "*QÂDASH*" or "*KADASH*" – mean "to sanctify, make holy, consecrate, separate."

> "There is no one holy (*KADOSH*) like *YHWH* (the LORD,) Indeed, there is no one besides You, Nor is there any rock like our *ELOHIM* (God.)" (1 Samuel 2:2, NASB95 Author's translation added)

Holiness is perhaps the most fundamental attribute of God.
Author Nathan Stone wrote in "*The Names of God*":

> "It is this holiness of which an old Scottish divine writes: 'It is the balance of all the attributes of deity. Power without holiness would degenerate into cruelty; omniscience without holiness would become craft; justice without holiness would degenerate into revenge; and goodness without holiness would be passionate and intemperate fondness doing mischief rather than accomplishing good.' It is this holiness which gives to God grandeur and majesty and, more than anything else, constitutes His fullness and perfection." (Stone 2010)[21]

Only God is holy and perfect. Yet, we are faced with this admonition to be holy and several others like it:

> "For I am *YHWH* (the LORD) your *ELOHIM* (God.) Consecrate (*KADASH*) yourselves therefore, and be holy (*KADOSH*), for I am holy (*KADOSH*)..." (Leviticus 11:44a, NASB95 Author's translation added)

If only God can be perfect (holy) then how can I "be holy"?
To make matters worse, Peter brought this command right into the context of the New Testament.

"As obedient children, do not be conformed to the former lusts which were yours in your ignorance, but like the Holy One who called you, be holy yourselves also in all your behavior; because it is written, 'YOU SHALL BE HOLY, FOR I AM HOLY.'" (1 Peter 1:14–16, NASB95)

Actually, a key aspect of *being* holy means being set apart or separated. To sanctify is the act of dedicating or setting apart for a purpose. God said to His chosen people, "Consecrate yourselves."

"You shall consecrate (*KADASH*) yourselves therefore and be holy (*KODESH*) for I am *YHWH* (the LORD) your *ELOHIM* (God). You shall keep My statutes and practice them; I am the LORD who sanctifies (*KADASH*) you (I am Yahweh- M'Kaddesh)." (Leviticus 20:7–8, NASB95 Author's translation added)

I understand here that *KADASH* is not exactly M'Kaddesh, but I'm not exactly a Hebrew scholar either. Hebrew verbs have stems and tenses that are apparent in the written Hebrew text but are hard, if not impossible, to reproduce exactly in English. For the purposes of this material, let's assume that M'Kaddesh fulfills the intention of the sentence from "YHWH sanctifies" to "I am YHWH who sanctifies you."

It may seem an impossible task to live up to the admonition to "be holy as I am holy." In truth, it is. How can I "sanctify" myself? First, I can guard my own life and how I live it. I can strive to honor Yahweh-M'Kaddesh with my words and deeds. I can obey Him by loving Him and loving others. I do have a role to play. But – and this is *the* "but" of all buts – it's Yahweh-M'Kaddesh who sanctifies us. It's Yahweh-M'Kaddesh who sets us apart from the world and brings us into His family. He replaces our best efforts with those of Jesus. He seals us with His Spirit who lives within us. And, if we are to be His sanctuary, we must first be sanctified. Yahweh-M'Kaddesh is trustworthy to do just what He said He would. Yahweh-M'Kaddesh. God who sets us apart.

I AM your Sanctifier.

He is Yahweh-Shammah

Pronunciation: yah-way′ – shah-mah′

In 930 BC, the united nation of Israel divided into two kingdoms: Israel with its capital of Samaria to the north, Judah with its capital of Jerusalem to the south. Solomon's Temple was of course in Jerusalem; therefore God's "dwelling" was in the temple in Jerusalem. His "presence" was actually there (but I doubt God actually lived completely in the temple). Think of His presence there in the same way you consider His presence in you as Holy Spirit. He is omnipresent, after all.

People who call themselves "deists" believe God created the universe then went on a permanent vacation. God is not on vacation! We worship a God who is present with us always.

His visible presence was called the "shekinah glory." Shekinah means "dwelling" or "one who dwells." Although this Hebrew word does not appear in the Old or New Testaments, Jewish rabbis first introduced it during the period between the two testaments to describe what the people experienced when they saw God's glory.

> "Now when Solomon had finished praying, fire came down from heaven and consumed the burnt offering and the sacrifices, and the glory (*KABOD*) of *YHWH* (the Lord) filled the house. The priests could not enter into the house of the Lord because the glory (*KABOD*) of the Lord filled the Lord's house. All the sons of Israel, seeing the fire come down and the glory (*KABOD*) of the Lord upon the house, bowed down on the pavement with their faces to the ground, and they worshiped and gave praise to the Lord, saying, 'Truly He is good, truly His lovingkindness is everlasting.'" (2 Chronicles 7:1–3, NASB95 Author's translation added)

"*KABOD*" is translated most often as "glory" or "honor." These rabbis would have used the Hebrew word "*SHEKINAH*" to describe what the priests saw on the day Solomon's Temple was dedicated. It was literally "YHWH's dwelling glory" or YHWH's shekinah glory. The term demonstrated that YHWH was present in the lives of Israel from the time of the exodus when He descended to Mount Sinai (Exodus 19:16–18), to when He led them in pillars of cloud and fire (Exodus 13:21–22), to when He covered and filled the tabernacle and beyond.

> "Then the cloud covered the tent of meeting, and the glory of the Lord filled the tabernacle. Moses was not able to enter the tent of meeting because

the cloud had settled on it, and the glory of the LORD filled the tabernacle." (Exodus 40:34–35, NASB95)

Later in Solomon's temple, His shekinah glory dwelt behind the veil in the Holy of Holies. But because of Judah's continued disobedience, God departed the temple and let His people be overrun by the Babylonians; the temple and all of Jerusalem were destroyed. The nation was divided, and both Israel and Judah were taken into captivity. But through Ezekiel, God sent a prophesy of hope to His people (Ezekiel 48:35, NASB95). He promised a time when Israel would be restored and know prosperity and security once again. It was a promise of a New Jerusalem, a new city. In the last verse in Ezekiel's book he says, "And the name of the city shall be, The LORD is There. Yahweh-Shammah."

Go back for a minute to the 2 Chronicles scripture above. Take note of the priests' response to seeing in person the manifested presence of YHWH. They bowed down with their faces in the dust. They "worshiped and gave praise to YHWH." Instead of trembling at the fiery spectacle of His glory, they simply said, "Truly He is good, truly His lovingkindness is everlasting." How would you respond to such a sight?

Our God has promised that He will be with us and never forsake us. That we can live in His presence forever! He didn't make us this promise because He has nothing better to do, but because He is good, truly good, and because He loves us. He truly loves you. So, let your response to His presence be worship. Yahweh-Shammah.

I AM with you.

He is Yahweh-Shalom

Pronunciation: yah-way' – shah-lōm'

At the time this name was given, Israel was in the period of the judges when they cycled (and recycled) from being in God's favor, to moving gradually away from Him, to God's punishing them, then His convicting and restoring them through a judge. A biblical judge was a ruler or military leader who presided over legal hearings. During a period when Israel was being oppressed by the Midianites, God revealed Himself to a young man named Gideon. God had heard Israel's cry for help and would restore the nation and bring peace through Judge Gideon, a man afraid and unsure that he was right for the job. But God persisted and addressed Gideon's fears with the word, peace. *SHALOM.*

> "When Gideon saw that he was the angel of *YHWH* (the Lord), he said, 'Alas, O *ADONAI* (Lord) *YHWH* (God)! For now I have seen the angel of *YHWH* (the Lord) face to face.' *YHWH* (The Lord) said to him, 'Peace (shalom) to you, do not fear; you shall not die.' Then Gideon built an altar there to *YHWH* (the Lord) and named it <u>The Lord is Peace</u> (Yahweh-Shalom)." (Judges 6:22–24, NASB95 Author's translation added)

Shalom is a familiar word. Israelis to this day greet one another with "Shalom," perhaps because they have had so little of it. Peace is not a cure-all, but it does seem to satisfy and soothe over a multitude of problems today. We all want peace on earth but, even more than that, we just want peace in our own hearts and minds.

Yahweh-Shalom. We can always find peace in God.

> "In peace I will both lie down and sleep, For You alone, O Lord, make me to dwell in safety." (Psalm 4:8, NASB95)

There is peace in safety and peace in provision. There is peace in the fact that my Adonai, my master, will protect me. I find great peace in knowing that the Elohim, the God of creation, desires a covenant relationship with me which He made possible through the provision of Jesus Christ. To His disciples, He said:

"Peace I leave with you; My peace I give to you; not as the world gives do I give to you. Do not let your heart be troubled, nor let it be fearful." (John 14:27, NASB95)

"Abide in Me, and I in you… I am the vine, you are the branches; he who abides in Me and I in him, he bears much fruit…" (John 15:4a–5a, NASB95)

We are often like the Israelites during the time of the judges. We cycle from having a close and intimate daily relationship with Abba, living in obedience to Him, and then gradually slipping away into our own selves. My quiet time gives way to busyness and business. My thought-life slips to thoughts of lust or greed or selfishness. I slowly – almost imperceptibly – find myself away from God. I didn't mean to go there, but here I am. Israel had to hit rock-bottom before they realized where they were in relation to YHWH. We may have to bottom out as well. But, as God's people, we can always cry out to Him, confess, and repent. Jesus is our Gideon – our Judge. He understands our plight but will never let us languish in our separation or self-pity. He wants us always to remain in close fellowship with the Father through Him.

"You did not choose Me but I chose you, and appointed you that you would go and bear fruit, and that your fruit would remain…" (John 15:16a, NASB95)

"These things I have spoken to you, so that in Me you may have peace. In the world you have tribulation, but take courage; I have overcome the world." (John 16:33, NASB95)

"Be anxious for nothing, but in everything by prayer and supplication with thanksgiving let your requests be made known to God. And the peace of God, which surpasses all comprehension, will guard your hearts and your minds in Christ Jesus." (Philippians 4:6–7, NASB95)

We are never closer to God, never more at peace, than when we worship Him as Yahweh-Shalom. Yahweh is Peace.

I AM your Peace.

He is Yahweh-Tsidkenu

Pronunciation: yah-way′ – sid-kay′-noo

God had made a promise to King David:

> ... "If your sons are careful of their way, to <u>walk before Me in truth</u> with all their heart and with all their soul, you shall not lack a man on the throne of Israel." (1 Kings 2:4, NASB95)

But David's sons did not keep their part of this covenant, and Israel experienced a long succession of bad kings. Fortunately, Jeremiah prophesied of a time when the security of Israel would not depend on the righteousness of her wicked kings.

> "'Behold, the days are coming,' declares the LORD, 'When I will raise up for David a righteous Branch; And He will reign as king and act wisely and do justice and righteousness in the land. In His days Judah will be saved, And Israel will dwell securely; And this is His name by which He will be called, <u>'The LORD our righteousness</u> (Yahweh Tsidkenu).'" (Jeremiah 23:5–6, NASB95 Author's translation added)

Who is this "righteous Branch" of David that Jeremiah is speaking of? Jesus, of course. He was in the direct lineage of David, thus the "branch of David." A "righteous" branch.

"Righteous" is another one of those words that has been highjacked by the world. Today it can mean "genuine or excellent." "Hey Dude, that was a righteous sauce!" (Guy Fieri, *Diners, Drive-ins, and Dives*)

However, even in the context of the Bible, righteousness can be a confusing concept.

> "Now when Abram was ninety-nine years old, *YHWH* (the LORD) appeared to Abram and said to him, 'I am El Shaddai (God Almighty); <u>Walk before Me, and be blameless.</u>'" (Genesis 17:1, NASB95 Author's translation added)

Here God uses the metaphor of "walking" before Him or in His presence. It simply means to "live out your life." Walking is something we all do as part of everyday life. And, even if you can't walk, you still understand the metaphor. "Walk before Me" translates to live out your life before me and "be blameless." Live without sin or as not guilty before God. I'm probably explaining something that is obvious but bear with me. I need to make a point: God expected Abram to live his everyday life before Him without sinning. While a "righteous" goal for God to set, sinlessness was not really practical for a fleshly human being. In fact, Abraham proved time and time again not to be righteous (blameless).

Yet, God used Abraham mightily in building His chosen people.

> "Then he (Abraham) believed in the LORD; and He reckoned it to him as righteousness." (Genesis 15:6, NASB95 Author's translation added)

> "Was not Abraham our father justified by works when he offered up Isaac his son on the altar? You see that faith was working with his works, and as a result of the works, faith was perfected; and the Scripture was fulfilled which says, 'AND ABRAHAM BELIEVED GOD, AND IT WAS RECKONED TO HIM AS RIGHTEOUSNESS,' and he was called the friend of God." (James 2:21–23, NASB95)

So, we see both from the Old Testament and the New that we have some responsibility for our righteousness before God. God expects us to walk before Him and, to the best of our abilities, be blameless.

This sounds like the same argument for "Be holy, for I am holy" that I made in Yahweh-M'Kaddesh. But holiness is more about being set apart from sin and the world's ways for God's own purposes. Righteousness is "right living" and being in "right relationship with God." It's more about living up to a standard set by God.

Under the Old Covenant, God "reckoned" Abraham's faith and his obedience (works) as righteousness, and He *reconciled* Abraham's account with Him based on these things. We could tell the same story about King David. With all of David's many sins, he was still blessed of God in so many ways. Yet, righteous remains an absolute. *There is no gray scale for God's righteous standard of living.* So, what do we do? Go back now to…

> "Behold, the days are coming," declares the LORD, "When I will raise up for David a righteous Branch." (Jer. 23:5 NASB95)

God saw ahead and made a provision for our sinful nature. That provision is, of course, Jesus. He is our example and power for walking blameless before God. Because of Jesus, we know what blameless looks like. But He also reconciled our accounts before a holy and righteous God, once and for all. And that reconciliation is still based on our faith in the living Christ.

"Therefore if anyone is in Christ, he is a new creature; the old things passed away; behold, new things have come. Now all these things are from God, who <u>reconciled us to Himself through Christ</u> and gave us the ministry of reconciliation, namely, that God was in Christ reconciling the world to Himself, <u>not counting their trespasses against them</u>, and He has committed to us the word of reconciliation. Therefore, we are ambassadors for Christ, as though God were making an appeal through us; we beg you on behalf of Christ, be reconciled to God. He made Him who knew no sin to be sin on our behalf, so <u>that we might become the righteousness of God in Him</u>." (2 Corinthians 5:17–21, NASB95)

God has made for us a way to be righteous in His eyes! Our response, our obligation, is first to accept our calling as His ambassadors to the world to bring the good news of His reconciliation. Then, to worship Him as we recognize and acknowledge His amazing grace.

> Amazing grace, how sweet the sound
> That saved a wretch like me
> I once was lost, but now I am found
> Was blind, but now I see.[36]
> **I AM your Righteousness.**

He is Yahweh-Y'ireh

Alternate: Jehovah-Jireh

Pronunciation: yah-way' – ye-rah-aah' (or Jī'-rah)

The word we write here as Y'ireh is difficult for the English speaker. The Hebrew root word is "*RAAH*" spoken with two syllables, rah-aah'. It's used hundreds of times in the Old Testament and translated many different ways, but the basic meaning is "to see" or "to see ahead." The transliteration from the context in Genesis 22 becomes Y'ireh which communicates "will provide." Because of this linguistic difficulty, many English speakers have deferred to Jehovah-Jireh.

When you think back over your entire life, including today, what are some special places in your memories? A place that you love to be. A favorite place. Maybe a place you played as child. A place you vacationed. A place where you experienced God.

In my retirement, I have taken up fly fishing. It's easily one of most difficult ways to catch a fish. But I have discovered that catching trout is only half the joy of fly fishing. The other half is standing there in that cold rushing water, with all the right equipment, in a beautiful, peaceful place, alone in God's creation that I find the most joy.

> "Many men go fishing all of their lives without knowing that it is not fish they are after." (Henry David Thoreau)

The Bible teaches that *places* are important to God. We see the importance of places beginning in Genesis when God created the Garden of Eden. When He called Abraham to the Promised Land. Mount Sinai, Canaan, and Jerusalem are all special places to God. In the Revelation we see Jesus establish the new Jerusalem that will be our eternal home. We even see God described as a place.

> "You are my hiding place…" (Psalm 32:7, NASB95)
> "Lord, You have been our dwelling place in all generations." (Psalm 90:1, NASB95)

It's appropriate that this name of God is also a place, a place named by Abraham for a characteristic God revealed to him there. But this place is not just Abraham's place. This place, and this name of God, is one He wants all of us to know first-hand!

> "Abraham called the name of that place The Lord Will Provide…(Yahweh-Y'ireh)." (Genesis 22:14, NASB95 Author's translation added)

YHWH-Y'ireh. YHWH will provide.

YHWH wants to be our provider. But, in real life, He has lots of competition.

One false provider is our *flesh*. We can let our flesh provide for our wants and needs. Along with it comes things like jealousy, anger, arguing, bitterness, selfishness, complaining, laziness, lust, perfectionism, and on and on.

Another counterfeit provider is *Satan*. He eagerly provides lies, accusations, fears, guilt, anxieties, discouragement, defeat, and depression.

Another human provider is the *world*. It provides pride, position, possessions, entertainment, materialism, greed, and godlessness.

These providers constantly pursue us, calling us, enticing us, seducing us, offering us what they have to give, and we're free to choose them. In fact, all we must do is do nothing, and they will become our default providers.

They're obviously not the provider God wants us to have.

As our Adonai, He wants to be our *only* provider and master.

> "You shall not worship them or serve them (other gods); for I, the Lord your God, am a jealous God..." (Exodus 20:5, NASB95 Author's translation added)

He wants us to refuse to accept anything these "other gods" have to offer. Instead, He wants us to look to Him and receive from Him our every need, because what He provides will always be for His glory and our good. He is sufficient. El Shaddai.

I have teased around and alluded to the Genesis story that follows several times. Abraham has served as our example as I've talked about his successes and failures. Now, read these verses through and take note of the words I have underlined.

> "Now it came about after these things, that God <u>tested</u> Abraham, and said to him, 'Abraham!' And he said, '<u>Here I am</u>.' He said, 'Take now <u>your son, your only son</u>, whom you <u>love</u>, Isaac, and go to the land of <u>Moriah</u>, and offer him there as a <u>burnt offering</u> on one of the mountains of which I will tell you.' So Abraham rose early in the morning and saddled his donkey, and took two of his young men with him and Isaac his son; and he split wood for the burnt offering, and arose and went to <u>the place</u> of which God had told him. On the third day Abraham raised his eyes and saw <u>the place</u> from a distance. Abraham said to his young men, 'Stay here with the donkey, and I and the lad will go over there; and <u>we will worship and return to you</u>.' Abraham took the wood of the burnt offering and laid it on Isaac his son, and he took in his hand the fire and the knife.

So, the two of them walked on together. Isaac spoke to Abraham his father and said, 'My father!' And he said, 'Here I am, my son.' And he said, 'Behold, the fire and the wood, but <u>where is the lamb</u> for the burnt offering?' Abraham said, '<u>God will provide for Himself the lamb</u> for the burnt offering, my son.' So, the two of them walked on together. Then they came to <u>the place</u> of which God had told him; and Abraham built <u>the altar</u> there and arranged the wood and bound his son Isaac and laid him on the altar, on top of the wood. Abraham stretched out his hand and took the knife to slay his son. But the Messenger (angel) of YHWH (the LORD) called to him from heaven and said, 'Abraham, Abraham!' And he said, '<u>Here I am.</u>' He said, 'Do not stretch out your hand against the lad, and do nothing to him; for now I know that you fear God, since you have not withheld your son, <u>your only son</u>, from Me.'

Then Abraham raised his eyes and looked, and behold, behind him a ram caught in the thicket by his horns; and Abraham went and took the ram and offered him up for a burnt offering <u>in the place of his son</u>. Abraham called the name of <u>that place The LORD Will Provide</u> (YHWH Y'ireh) as it is said to this day, '<u>In the mount of the LORD it will be provided.</u>'

Then the angel of the LORD called to Abraham a second time from heaven, and said, 'By Myself I have sworn, declares the LORD, because you have done this thing and have not withheld your son, your only son, indeed I will greatly bless you, and I will greatly multiply your seed as the stars of the heavens and as the sand which is on the seashore; and your seed shall possess the gate of their enemies. In <u>your seed</u> all the nations of the earth shall be <u>blessed</u>, because you have obeyed My voice.'

So, Abraham returned to his young men, and they arose and went together to Beersheba; and Abraham lived at Beersheba." (Genesis 22:1–19, NASB95 Author's translation added)

This incredible story is one of the greatest and most significant passages in the Bible. The narrative tells of a literal event in the life of Abraham and Isaac that happened around 2,000 BC. But (as is much of the Old Testament) this story is also a portrait drawn by God for us of The Christ who is to come. A foreshadowing of God's greatest provision offered freely to us through His sacrifice of Christ on the cross. While this passage speaks about many things, it can best be summarized like this:

God saves Isaac through the provision of a substitute.

> ....and Abraham went and took the ram, and offered him up for a burnt offering *in the place of* his son...

The key words here are "in the place of." The sacrifice was still necessary but, instead of requiring Isaac's life as a sacrifice or payment for sin, God provided a ram.

Many years ago, Paul Harvey, a highly respected journalist, hosted a syndicated radio program called *The Rest of the Story*. The show began as a narrative that set the stage for a fascinating surprise ending. Harvey always closed the show with his patented phrase, "Now you know the *rest* of the story."

Genesis 22:1–19 is just the narrative to set up the story.

This same Mount Moriah became the hill where the city of Jerusalem would be built. And, about 1,000 years after Abraham, on a rocky plateau just north of Jerusalem, Solomon built on this site his magnificent temple for the glory and worship of YHWH. This temple with its stone and bronze altar was the center of the Jewish sacrificial system for hundreds of years. Still today this area is called "The Temple Mount." Then, about 2,000 years after Abraham built *his* altar here, on this same high rocky area, God offered the final substitute sacrifice for sin, once and for all, as payment for our transgressions. This part of Mount Moriah was later called Mount Calvary or the Place of the Skull.

John 3:16 says, "God so loved the world that He gave <u>His only begotten Son...</u>" (NASB95)

Romans 8:32 says He "spared not <u>his only Son</u> but delivered him up for us all." (NASB95)

John 1:20 says of Jesus, "Behold <u>the Lamb of God</u>, which takes away the sin of the world." (NASB95)

So, Genesis 22 shows us that God has provided for our <u>sins</u>.

"In the mount of the LORD *it* will be provided."

He will be provided. Yahweh-Y'ireh. Jehovah-Jireh.

Now we know the *rest* of the story. Or do we...

We also see here that "Yahweh will provide" for *all* our needs – spiritual, physical, and emotional – through our ongoing relationship with Jesus Christ. Let's think about just *who* is Yahweh-Y'ireh (Jehovah Jireh)? *How* does He operate? *When* is His provision given to us? *What* do we have to do for Him to give us what we need? *What* type of provider is Yahweh-Y'ireh? And *how* can we personally know Him and trust Him by this name?

Here are a few principles for understanding how and when Yahweh provides.

1. *Provision will follow **tests** from God.*

Genesis 22:1 (NASB95) says God *tested* Abraham. Now most of us don't like tests. But tests of our faith are part of Yahweh-Y'ireh's plan for us. So, we must learn to accept them with understanding and joy.

> "Consider it all joy, my brethren, when you encounter various trials, knowing that the testing of your faith produces endurance. And let endurance have its perfect result, so that you may be perfect and complete, <u>lacking in nothing</u>." (James 1:2–4, NASB95)

2. *Provision will follow **obedience** to God.*

Roger Mardis, a pastor friend, used to say, "I want to be under the spout when the blessings come out!" (Well, that's my version of what he said.) But there's a world of truth in that statement, and the best way to be under God's "spout of provision" is by obeying what He tells us to do. If He tells us *not* to forsake our assembling together in church, then He has something He wants to provide for us there. If He tells us to meditate on His Word daily, then He has something He wants to impart to us through His Word. If He tells us to forgive someone else, then He has a blessing He wants to give us as we obey.

Abraham obeyed God and Isaac obeyed Abraham when they walked 50 miles on foot to Mount Moriah. When young Isaac asked his father, "Where is the lamb for the burnt offering?" Abraham said, "God will provide for Himself the lamb…" Abraham knew and trusted YHWH to provide everything.

Let me say one thing, strongly, here to avoid misunderstanding. We do not *earn* our salvation; it is a gift of God, received on the basis of our faith and repentance. God's love for us is unconditional. But many of His promises and blessings are conditional, based on our obedience.

3. *Provision will follow **communication** with God.*

This communication can also be called "prayer."

In Genesis 22, Abraham was a man who listened to God's voice (verse 18). His life's attitude was, "Here I am, Lord. Waiting to hear from You. Waiting to do what You want me to do." You see this in verses 1 and 11.

Did Abraham's life of trust and prayer happen overnight? Was he always directed toward God's voice, dependent on His guidance, discerning of what God wanted him to do? Definitely not. Look at Genesis 16:2. At the end, it says...and Abram listened to the voice of Sarai, his wife (NASB95). You can read this story in the section on El-Roi. Abraham wasn't led by God at that point. He provided for his needs through his flesh, through Satan, or the world. And, as a result, he fathered Ismael through an adulterous relationship, and he got himself – and the world – in a lot of trouble.

God's Word teaches that as we pray, listen to God, and ask Him for our needs, He will provide. And we *will* receive.

> "Why do you spend money for what is not bread, and your wages for what does not satisfy? Listen carefully to Me, and eat what is good, and delight yourself in abundance. Incline your ear and come to Me. Listen, that you may live; And I will make an everlasting covenant with you, according to the faithful mercies shown to David." (Isaiah 55:2–3, NASB95)

> "Ask, and it will be given to you; seek, and you will find; knock, and it will be opened to you. For everyone who asks receives, and he who seeks finds, and to him who knocks it will be opened. Or what man is there among you who, when his son asks for a loaf, will give him a stone? Or if he asks for a fish, he will not give him a snake, will he? If you then, being evil, know how to give good gifts to your children, how much more will your Father who is in heaven give what is good to those who ask Him!"(Matthew 7:7–11, NASB95)

Only in close communication with God will we most often receive His provision. Imagine, in verse 12, if Abraham – knife in hand – *hadn't listened to God*. Isaac would have been killed. And they (and perhaps we) would have missed God's greatest provision.

Earlier we saw that Y'ireh (or Jireh) means "to see." But it may be hard to understand what "to see' and "to provide" have in common.

"Y'ireh" actually communicates *"will* see" or "see *ahead.*" Our English word "see" comes from the Greek word "*VIDEO.*" Shortened it becomes "vide." Thus, pre-vide or pre-vision in English is to "see before" or "see ahead." So "provide" or "provision" involves "looking ahead that one might meet the needs of another." This kind of pre-vision describes our Yahweh-Y'ireh! Our God has seen ahead to provide everything we need. Not "God *did* provide" but "God *will* provide."

And what *will* God provide from Genesis 22? Not just a ram caught in the thicket by its horns, but deliverance and life for Isaac through a substitute! This pictures perfectly the substitutionary sacrifice of His Son, Jesus Christ. Instead of me on the altar of atonement, it was Jesus, there in my place.

How does Yahweh-Y'ireh provide for our everyday needs today? Again, through Jesus Christ, and through our relationship of love, worship, and obedience to Him.

Where is God's wonderful place of provision for you?

It's in testing and obedience and prayer.

It's in living the attitude of "Here I am, Lord. Whatever you have will be fine with me."

"In the mount of YHWH, it will be provided." (NASB95)

I encourage you to be in *that place* to receive God's provision.

That place can be discovered in worship of Yahweh-Y'ireh.

> "Blessed be the God and Father of our Lord Jesus Christ, who has <u>blessed us with every spiritual blessing</u> in the heavenly places in Christ," (Ephesians 1:3, NASB95)

> "And my God will <u>supply all your needs</u> according to His riches in glory in Christ Jesus. Now to our God and Father be the glory forever and ever. Amen." (Philippians 4:19–20, NASB95)

> "Now to Him who is able to <u>do far more abundantly beyond all that we ask</u> or think, according to the power that works within us, to Him be the glory in the church and in Christ Jesus to all generations forever and ever. Amen." (Ephesians 3:20–21, NASB95)

I AM your provider.
I AM sufficient.

He is Yahweh-Roh' i

Pronunciation: yah-way′ – rō′-hee

"The LORD is my shepherd; I shall not want." Maybe the most comforting and beautiful words in the Bible. And ones that include, I believe, the most understandable and reassuring name we might associate with our God.

I've admitted I grew up on a farm so I might have an advantage when it comes to understanding livestock and what it takes to raise them. I've fed the cows with bales of hay, I've slopped the hogs, I've even had a "hand in" helping artificially inseminate one of Daddy's Hereford heifers. (Don't look it up.) But I've never really been around sheep.

People have the idea that sheep aren't too smart, but none of the livestock on a farm are going to win any scholarships. On our farm we had lots of barbed wire fences. This kept the cows in and Mr. Johnson's bull out, at least until the agreed- upon springtime romantic rendezvous (remember the borrowed bull?). Still, it's easy enough for me and maybe you to picture the tasks that were before a shepherd in the days before barbed wire. It had to be difficult just to keep them from wandering away in a hundred different directions. Wolves are mentioned about a dozen times in the Bible and, most of the time, they are either an actual or a metaphorical enemy of the sheep. So, a shepherd had to "corral" the sheep somehow and be prepared to fight off an attacking wolf pack. His only real tool or weapon was a staff, a long stick with a crook at one end and maybe a sling. The sling took some practice, but it would propel a small, smooth stone at a wolf or maybe a robber. David, the shepherd boy, used a sling like this one against animals and one really big dude with great effect. I'll get to that in a minute.

The best shepherds were the owners of the flock or their sons. They worked harder and took greater risks to protect their investments and livelihoods. A "hireling," on the other hand, had less skin in the game and might lay down his staff and run away in a real pinch (like a wolf). No reason to risk your life for someone else's animals.

I hope you're forming a picture for yourself of the relationship between the shepherd and his sheep. The Bible is full of references to this relationship. Maybe the best one comes from the Old Testament chronicles of the young David.

You can read David's story in 1 Samuel 16, but here are the basics. The prophet Samuel was sent by God to Bethlehem to choose the new king of Israel from the sons of Jesse. David, the youngest son, was tending his father's sheep when Samuel arrived. After a parade of candidates, David was anointed that day as the future king. He was a young man at the time. In the meantime, the present king, Saul, came to hear about David because of his skills as a musician and his valor as a young warrior. David came into Saul's service, but also still served his father as shepherd.

In chapter 17 we see the famous battle lines drawn between the army of the Israelites and the army of the Philistines. The giant Goliath screamed out his taunts. Now, any kid who ever attended Sunday School knows the rest of this story. David went out armed only with his shepherd's staff, his sling, and a few smooth stones. When Goliath taunted David, he responded with these words:

> "…'You come to me with a sword, a spear, and a javelin, but I come to you in the name of YHWH *SABAOTH* (the Lord of hosts), the *ELOHIM* (God) of the armies of Israel, whom you have taunted. This day *YHWH* (the Lord) will deliver you up into my hands…'" (1 Samuel 17:45–46, NASB95 Author's translation added)

Young David trusted his skills, and he trusted his YHWH. I can see the shepherd boy and the giant now, displayed on Mrs. Tate's flannelgraph board in my Sunday School classroom back home. I dreamed of being like David, the shepherd boy. Today, I have a shepherd's staff and a sling with five smooth stones in my study.

OK, why all this stuff about farm animals and flannelgraph stories?

When I read David's Psalm # 23, I can really *believe* what he says:

> "The Lord is my shepherd; I shall not want. He maketh me to lie down in green pastures: He leadeth me beside the still waters. He restoreth my soul: He leadeth me in the paths of righteousness for his name's sake. Yea, though I walk through the valley of the shadow of death, I will fear no evil: for thou art with me; Thy rod and thy staff they comfort me. Thou preparest a table before me in the presence of mine enemies: Thou anointest my head with oil; my cup runneth over. Surely goodness and mercy shall follow me all the days of my life: And I will dwell in the house of the Lord forever." (Psalm 23:1–6, KJV)

I can also trust Jesus when He said…

> "I am the good shepherd; the good shepherd lays down His life for the sheep. He who is a hired hand, and not a shepherd, who is not the owner of the sheep, sees the wolf coming, and leaves the sheep and flees, and the wolf snatches them and scatters them. He flees because he is a hired hand and is not concerned about the sheep. I am the good shepherd, and I know My

own and My own know Me, even as the Father knows Me and I know the Father; and I lay down My life for the sheep. I have other sheep, which are not of this fold; I must bring them also, and they will hear My voice; and they will become one flock with one shepherd. For this reason the Father loves Me, because I lay down My life so that I may take it again." (John 10:11–17, NASB95)

When Jesus speaks of "My own" sheep, He is referring to the Jewish people. His own ethnic people. And when He speaks of these "other" sheep, He's talking about you and me. He laid down His life – as our Good Shepherd – for all of us. But the best news is He took it up again!

Allow me to tie up some loose ends before we get to the last name of God.

YHWH is my shepherd,
    Yahweh-Rohi – I AM your Shepherd.

I shall not want.
    Yahweh-Y'ireh – I AM your Provider.

He makes me lie down in green pastures; He leads me beside quiet waters.
    Yahweh-Shalom – I AM your Peace.

He restores my soul.
    Yahweh-Rophe – I AM your Healer.

He guides me in the paths of righteousness for His name's sake.
    Yahweh-Tsidkenu – I AM your Righteousness.

Even though I walk through the valley of the shadow of death, I fear no evil
    Adonai – I AM your Lord and Master.

for You are with me;
    Yahweh-Shammah – I AM with you.

Your rod and Your staff, they comfort me.
    Yahweh-Nissi – I AM your Banner.

You prepare a table before me in the presence of my enemies;
You have anointed my head with oil; My cup overflows.
    El Shaddai – I AM Sufficient.

Surely goodness and mercy will follow me all the days of my life,
    Yahweh-M'Kaddesh – I AM your Sanctifier.

And I will dwell in the house of YHWH forever.
    Elohim – I AM the Great God of Creation and Covenant.
    I AM your Shepherd.

(Author's translation)

He is Yeshua Hamashiach

Pronunciation: yesh-hoo'-ah ha-mah-she'-akkh
Alternate: Yehoshua or Joshua
English Transliteration: Jesus Christ

"... the angel Gabriel was sent from God to a city in Galilee called Nazareth, to a virgin ... and the virgin's name was Mary." (Luke 1:26–27, NASB95)

"And behold, you will conceive in your womb and bear a son, and you shall name Him Jesus. He will be great and will be called the Son of the Most High..." (Luke 1:31–32, NASB95)

"And Joseph her husband ... an angel of the Lord appeared to him in a dream, saying, 'Joseph, son of David, do not be afraid to take Mary as your wife; for the Child who has been conceived in her is of the Holy Spirit. She will bear a Son; and you shall call His name Jesus, for He will save His people from their sins.' Now all this took place to fulfill what was spoken by the Lord through the prophet: 'BEHOLD, THE VIRGIN SHALL BE WITH CHILD AND SHALL BEAR A SON, AND THEY SHALL CALL HIS NAME IMMANUEL,' which translated means, 'GOD WITH US.'" (Matthew 1:19–23, NASB95) (ISAIAH 7:14)

Some of the names we have studied were given to God by His servants as they discovered something wonderful about Him. Others were given to God by Himself to reveal His character to His servants and to us. So much of God's nature and character are revealed to us by these marvelous Old Testament names.

But now, here we are transitioning into the New Testament. We see this messenger from God announcing to this frightened, young, unmarried couple that they will conceive, not by natural means, but by the supernatural! With this revelation, he tells them exactly what to name the baby boy. His name would be Yeshua, which means "He will save His people from their sins." This name was prophesy in itself! But, if that weren't enough, this angelic creature quotes the Prophet Isaiah from 700 years before: "BEHOLD, THE VIRGIN SHALL BE WITH CHILD AND SHALL BEAR A SON, AND THEY SHALL CALL HIS NAME IMMANUEL."

Matthew, the gospel writer, provides the translation for this new Hebrew name IMMANUEL. "God with us."

Not Elohim, the great and mighty Creator.

Not El Shaddai, the All Sufficient One.

Not even Yahweh-Shammah – I AM There.

No. Now, God is *here*. Right here with us, *one of us*.

The Old Testament prophets brought many prophesies from God to His people; the most notable ones foretell of a "chosen one." Remember the story of young David when he was chosen by God to be king? Samuel, to signify this status, anointed David's head with oil. The Jewish people to this day have long awaited the appearance of an "Anointed One." The Hebrew word for Anointed One is "*MASHIACH*." We call him Messiah. Of course, many religions and peoples have expected *their* messiah to save them from whatever. Hundreds of Old Testament prophesies speak of the Jewish Messiah. I'd encourage you to read Isaiah 53. Look for the references that line up with who Jesus was and what He did for us. This chapter may be the best of the many messianic O.T. scriptures.

But it was not "a" messiah that was expected, but "THE" Messiah. "*HA*" *MASHIACH*.

Yeshua Hamashiach. Jesus The Messiah. Now allow the New Testament writers to translate this name into Greek, and we see *YESHUA*, the *CHRISTOS*. Jesus (the) Christ. Yeshua is the Hebrew name that we now pronounce as "Jesus."

Jesus or Yeshua was not an uncommon name for the time. But for *this* particular Jesus, the name brought with it a dire responsibility that no child should have to grow up with. How would this little boy ever save His people?

And yet He did. If anyone ever "owned" His name it was *this* Jesus. He grew up knowing who He was and what His mission must be. He was 30 years old before the mission began with His baptism by His cousin John and His infilling by Holy Spirit, His "biological" father. (Can that be right?) None the less, He surrounded Himself with 12 unremarkable men and went about His business – to "save His people from their sins."

But how would *anyone* go about accomplishing such an impossible task? He was the son of a carpenter, for goodness' sake. How could He preach enough gospel sermons or baptize enough repentant people to save the world? One man, with 12 everyday Joes following Him around? Of course, the answer lay in the ancient way that God had established all those centuries before. A blood sacrifice.

Volumes have been written about who Jesus was and what He has done for "His people" (and all the rest of us). So, I will not endeavor to recount any of that, other than to say this: Jesus was the once-and-for-all blood sacrifice who satisfied the penalty for all my sins and yours. "*Through*" this sacrifice I am saved! "*Through*" the cross I have access to the Father! "*Through*" Jesus I can enter into the very presence of Elohim and give Him praise!

**With the help of the Holy Spirit, we will worship The Father
through Jesus.**

To fully understand and appreciate what Jesus has done for us, I will allow the Word of God to speak for Himself.

"I am the bread of life; he who comes to Me will not hunger, and he who believes in Me will never thirst." (John 6:35, NASB95)

"I am the Light of the world; he who follows Me will not walk in the darkness but will have the Light of life." (John 8:12, NASB95)

"I am the door; if anyone enters through Me, he will be saved, and will go in and out and find pasture." (John 10:9, NASB95)

"I am the good shepherd; the good shepherd lays down His life for the sheep. I am the good shepherd, and I know My own and My own know Me," (John 10:11, 14, NASB95)

"I am the resurrection and the life; he who believes in Me will live even if he dies, and everyone who lives and believes in Me will never die. Do you believe this?" (John 11:25–26, NASB95)

"I am the way, and the truth, and the life; no one comes to the Father but through Me." (John 14:6, NASB95)

"Believe Me that I am in the Father and the Father is in Me; otherwise believe because of the works themselves." (John 14:11, NASB95)

"I am the true vine, and My Father is the vinedresser."

"I am the vine, you are the branches; he who abides in Me and I in him, he bears much fruit, for apart from Me you can do nothing." (John 15:1, 5, NASB95)

"Truly, truly, I say to you, before Abraham was born, I am." (John 8:58, NASB95)

His name is Master, Savior, Lion of Judah,
Blessed Prince of Peace,
Shepherd, Fortress, Rock of Salvation, Lamb of God Is He.
Son of David, King of the Ages, Eternal Life,
Holy Lord of Glory, His name is Life.[37]
    by Carman, Gloria Gaither and Bill Gaither

His name is wonderful; His name is wonderful;
His name is wonderful, Jesus my Lord.
He is the mighty King, Master of everything,
His name is wonderful, Jesus my Lord.
Bow down before Him; Love and adore Him;
His name is wonderful, Jesus my Lord.
He's the great Shepherd,
The Rock of all ages, almighty God is He.[38]
    by Audrey Mieir

Turn your eyes upon Jesus.
Look full in His wonderful face.
And the things of earth will grow strangely dim
In the light of His glory and grace.[39]
    by Steven Taylor & Helen Lemmel

8

ROMANS CHAPTER 12 VERSE 1

"Therefore, I urge you, brethren, by the mercies of God, to present your bodies a living and holy sacrifice, acceptable to God, which is your spiritual service of worship." (Romans 12:1, NASB95)

"And so, dear brothers and sisters, I plead with you to give your bodies to God because of all he has done for you. Let them be a living and holy sacrifice—the kind he will find acceptable. This is truly the way to worship him" (Romans 12:1, NLT)

Most any serious Christian has memorized this verse of scripture. (If you have not, get busy and do it now.)

Right here, the NASB Bible speaks about "your spiritual service of worship." About "presenting a sacrifice," an "acceptable" sacrifice. So, in a book about worship, we'd better dig into

> *Stand true to God and he will bring out his truth in a way that will make your life an expression of worship.*
>
> – OSWALD CHAMBERS

this verse a bit just to make sure we understand what it means and how it affects our worship.

Paul starts with, "Therefore." When any verse starts with "therefore," we need to find out what the "therefore" is there for. In Romans 11, he talks about the "mercies of God," His wisdom and knowledge, His judgments, and unfathomable ways. The chapter ends with "To Him be the glory forever. Amen."

Therefore, with all these wonderful attributes of God in mind, Paul urges us, he strongly *persuades* us, to present our bodies as a living and holy sacrifice. Our bodies, our whole selves! Not just our feet or hands or voice or mind, but our whole self. All that we are, holding nothing back. The animal sacrificed in temple worship was killed, cut into pieces, and placed on the altar to be burned. What if a priest held back a choice piece of the beef for himself when he was not allowed to? God wanted the fire to consume the entire sacrifice and did not tolerate any priest's selfish behavior.

Today, God wants us alive and whole! He has plans and purposes for us if we will just offer our whole selves to Him. He wants every part, including the very best parts. And not just *whole*, but *holy*! The sacrificial animal had to be unblemished, not the skinny or spotted goat, but the pure, white lamb. The best His people had to offer. "Holy" means "set apart," not perfect. God wants all of us, set apart for His purposes, the best we have to offer.

In this book, we use the visual of building an altar in our practice of worship. We incorporate **attitudes**, **acts**, and **acknowledgements** of worship, pictured as "STONES" with which we build our worship altar each day. We choose these stones freely in our worship, as God leads. We can choose several stones and "stack them up" in a way that represents our worship at that time, in that situation.

I trust this visualization technique is helpful. But we might take it one step further. When you build your daily altar for worship, consider climbing up on it yourself. (Slow down and let that sink in.) Consider presenting your whole self as a living and holy sacrifice as your "service of worship." As you do, think of Romans 12:1, and ask YHWH to take and use *all* of you this day for His glory.

Jesus did exactly this same thing. His altar was the cross. He did it voluntarily. He was alive, set apart for God's purposes. He gave all He had to offer. As you consider how to "present your body as a living and holy sacrifice," you may want to memorize this verse as well:

> "I have been crucified with Christ; and it is no longer I who live, but Christ lives in me; and the life which I now live in the flesh I live by faith in the Son of God, who loved me and gave Himself up for me." (Galatians 2:20, NASB95)

In your worship, say this scripture out loud to God. Proclaim it as your own. "I have been crucified with Christ." (BTW, the Greek word for "I" is "*EGO*.")

> "Now if we have died with Christ, we believe that we shall also live with Him, knowing that Christ, having been raised from the dead, is never to die again; death no longer is master over Him. For the death that He died, He died to sin once for all; but the life that He lives, He lives to God. Even

so <u>consider yourselves to be dead to sin, but alive to God in Christ Jesus</u>."
(Romans 6:8–11, NASB95)

A living sacrifice can always crawl off the altar. Declare yourself to be "dead to sin, but alive to God in Christ Jesus." If we can truly identify with what Jesus did for us on His altar, then this whole "living sacrifice" thing becomes much more than just an intellectual exercise, just something we say or imagine. It becomes something we do. Romans 12:1 *is an act of worship.*

- I will live by faith in the Son of God.
- I will trust Him and not the world.
- I will act in a way that reflects Him in everything I do.
- I will obey His words to me.
- I will speak His name to others.
- I will conquer my own flesh and my own desires.
- I will live my whole life, every moment of it, in a way that is acceptable and well-pleasing to my Father.

If this surrendered life costs me the respect or friendship of others, then so be it. If I don't get promoted, or chosen, or honored, then I am willing to sacrifice these temporal things. I will live in a way that brings glory to God, my Abba, my Adonai, my Sanctifier, my Provider, my Creator.

At the end of the Last Supper, Jesus and His disciples had business to attend to. "And when they had sung a hymn, they went out…" (Mark 14:26, ESV).

All to Jesus I surrender, All to Him I freely give
I will ever love and trust Him, In His presence daily live.
I surrender all. I surrender all.
All to Thee my blessed Savior, I surrender all.[40]

You have business to attend to.
Get up and get on with Romans Chapter 12 Verse 1.

Greg Dixon

9

MUSIC AND SONGS IN WORSHIP

Music just might be God's second greatest gift to humankind. Think about it. Music is one of very few universal languages. It influences every culture, every geography, in all recorded history no matter the level of civilization or sophistication (or the lack thereof).

> *Worship: Where God isn't moved by the quality of our voice but by the condition of our hearts.*
>
> – CHRIS TOMLIN

Anthropologists call it a "cultural universal." There is quite a long list of these universals that don't interest me. There are two that do: music and religion.

The Bible says we were "created in God's image."

> "Then God said, 'Let Us make man in Our image, according to Our likeness...'" (Genesis 1:26a, NASB95)

It also says Jesus was the "exact representation of His (God's) nature." (Hebrews 1:3, NASB95 Author's translation added)

But, if God is spirit and has no "image" from which to create a "likeness," then what can this verse mean? I studied this question pretty thoroughly (15 or 20 minutes) and the answer is... I still don't really know. But I have a pretty good theory of my own, in case you're interested.

In our study of God, His nature, His character, and His names we have discovered much of who He is. And, as we carefully study the life of Jesus, we clearly see His character and nature. Jesus was God clothed in a man-suit. All God and all man. Now, with this more complete view of God, we can develop the idea that all people are indeed "like" God in many ways. You, me, and every person, saved and not, all bear some of His divine characteristics.

For instance, humankind, as a whole, seems to have an innate sense of what is right and wrong that lines up with God's laws. Laws like don't murder or steal or lie. Humans, overall, want to believe in some "higher power" who is above and beyond the human experience. We want to believe there is a life beyond this earthly one. We can see we all have these things in common, and they are qualities of God. So, if music is also a common and desired pursuit enjoyed by most humans, then my theory is that YHWH is, in fact, musical. Keep in mind that this inverse logic is my idea alone and would probably fail some theological test applied by an actual smart person. But I'm sticking with it. God likes music and that's why we like it as well. To quote a famous poet *and* a famous rock drummer, "Music is the language of heaven."[22]

Music and songs are two different things if you think about it. On the radio we hear "music" that we might call the tune or melody with a tempo and style that appeal to us (or not). And we hear the "lyrics" or words that we sing with a message or story we can relate to. Both parts of what we collectively call "music" – the notes and the words – can separately speak to a human being.

Think of the genius we hear in classical music. Mozart wrote music, one note at a time, with a quill pen and ink. How is it that a unique combination of tones can stir the soul to tears of joy? Well, I think *God in us* responds to music in some mysterious way. Music somehow resonates with our heartstrings and creates a harmony that is part of who God is and part of how we are made in His image. We like instrumental music because God does, because He invented it in the first place. (Just my theory.)

Then there are the lyrics. A unique combination of words that speak to us in ways that go far beyond the words themselves. The words sound "lyrical" with a meter and rhyme and flow, like music does. Lyrics express emotions in ways that are passionate and beautiful to the human heart and mind. They tell a story that communicates more than just the narrative. Songs become poetry. Now, consider the classical poets and poems.

> Whose woods these are I think I know.
> His house is in the village though;
> He will not see me stopping here
> To watch his woods fill up with snow.
>
> The woods are lovely, dark and deep,
> But I have promises to keep,
> And miles to go before I sleep,
> And miles to go before I sleep.
>   by Robert Frost

Poetry puts beautiful words in our hearts and minds, words that we often cannot express for ourselves. Poetry moves us.

Now put these two wonderful things together, music and poetry, and something magical happens! We cannot explain it, just enjoy it, a universal experience of pure pleasure. We can try to thank the composer, and musician, and poet, and lyricist, and singer for bringing these marvelous things to life for us. But the very talents they possess, I believe, are from YHWH Himself and meant for His people to enjoy as they express the glory of YHWH Himself.

The Bible is full of references to music and actual song lyrics written in response to YHWH, His character, and His actions. Jubal was the first musician mentioned (Genesis 4:21). He was considered the "father of all those who play the lyre and pipe" (NASB95). I won't debate here the length of time from Genesis to now (old earth vs. new earth) but, in any case, Jubal lived a long, long time ago. People have been strumming strings and blowing pipes and making music "forever."

The first song recorded in our Bible is in Exodus 15:1–18. God had parted the Red Sea and allowed for the escape from Egypt. Here is a bit of it.

> "Then Moses and the sons of Israel <u>sang</u> this song to *YHWH* (the LORD,) and said, 'I will sing to *YHWH*, for He is <u>highly exalted</u>; The horse and its rider He has hurled into the sea. *YHWH* is my strength and song, And He has become my salvation; This is my *ELOHIM*, and I will <u>praise</u> Him; My father's *ELOHIM*, and I will <u>extol</u> Him. *YHWH* is a warrior; *YHWH* <u>is His name</u>.'" (Exodus 15:1–3, NASB95 Author's translation added)

Moses's song goes on and on about the mighty deeds of YHWH, His holiness, His lovingkindness, and His strength. It ends with this…

> "*YHWH* shall reign forever and ever." (Exodus 15:18, NASB95 Author's translation added)

> "Miriam the prophetess, Aaron's sister, took the timbrel in her hand, and all the women went out after her with timbrels and with dancing.

> Miriam answered them, '<u>Sing</u> to *YHWH*, for He is <u>highly exalted</u>; The horse and his rider He has hurled into the sea.'" (Exodus 15:20–21, NASB95 Author's translation added)

Someone (likely Moses) wrote this song for the express purposes of worshiping YHWH. He wrote it down, in verse, and somehow copied it for the "choir" to see and sing along. The women sang, danced, and played tambourines. Moses was the first minister of music and Miriam, the first praise team leader.

YHWH's people SANG and EXALTED and PRAISED and extoled Him. Then they sang some more as they danced and played MUSIC. They REMEMBERED and ASCRIBED the mighty deeds that YHWH had performed on their behalf. They ACKNOWLEDGED His character and nature, and they PROCLAIMED His name. YHWH!! "Yahweh in His name!" *This is how God's people worshiped together.*

OK, I doubt that anyone reading this book needs to be convinced that music and song play a huge role in the worship of God. I don't care what kind of Bible-believing church you attend; music of some kind plays a key role in the "worship" service. We all enjoy singing along with our choir or worship leaders the words written in a hymnal or projected up on a screen (or maybe from memory). *Music is how God's people worship together.*

Well…maybe.

Just because you sing along with the choir, or even if you are *in* the choir, doesn't necessarily mean you are worshiping God. "Singing along" is not the same as "singing to." This coming Sunday, when you attend your church "worship" service, *actually worship.* Here's how…

First, is there some sin still glaring at you that you haven't dealt with? If so, then just stay in the car and send your family in ahead of you. Confess and repent of it. Remember, "clean hands and a pure heart." Then, as you sit there in the pew or theater chair waiting for things to start, make sure your attitudes are in order. Are you still foggy from staying up or out too late? Are you still mad that somebody in your family made you late? Are you a little too proud of your outfit? Are you mulling over who recognized you in the lobby and who didn't? Your attitudes before and during your church service will make all the difference in your worship experience. Start with humility and go from there. "Worship in spirit and in truth."

Now, don't just sing along.
Sing to YHWH, for He is highly exalted.
Sing the words *to Him.*

Amazing grace how sweet the sound,
That saved a wretch like me. [41]

My hope is built on nothing less
Than Jesus blood and righteousness. [42]

> *Rise up, YHWH, in all Your power. With music and singing we will celebrate Your mighty acts.*
>
> – DAVID BEN JESSE (Ps. 21:13, NLT)

Savior, He can move the mountains

My God is mighty to save, He is mighty to save. [43]

Now, change the third person pronouns to second person. And speak His name to Him.

"Savior, *You* can move the mountains."

"Yahweh is mighty to save, *You* are mighty to save."

Sing *to* God, not *about* Him. Worship *Him,* not the song or the singer. Sing to be heard by *Him*, not your neighbor. Make this your *true service of worship* (Romans 12:1).

One more thing and I'll get off my high horse.

Bring music into your private worship as well. Here are a few practical tools that might help.

- Your private worship time should be private. That way, no one can hear you sing out loud to God. You don't need to shout, but you can. You shouldn't have to worry about who's listening or if your voice sounds good or not so good. God will love it, no matter what.

- Use your smart phone, tablet, or laptop and find (or make) a playlist of worship songs you like. Most folks these days subscribe to a streaming music service like Apple Music, Spotify, or Amazon Music. Or maybe you're old-fashioned like me and still download digital songs from the Apple Store. Either way, do a little homework, and create a playlist of the worship songs you like. Make sure they are worship songs and not just songs you like. They should speak directly to God as well as suit your own tastes. Worship music is a subset of Christian music. If you like traditional hymns, that's fine, but you might be missing out on some really amazing music if you are a strict traditionalist (e.g., *I Can Only Imagine* by Mercy Me). And that advice works both ways. Millennials should Google "best loved hymns of all time" (e.g., *A Mighty Fortress is our God* by Martin Luther).

- Once you have a playlist of a couple of dozen songs, just press "shuffle." I do this because it allows Holy Spirit to choose the song for today. It always seems to work out better that way.

- Instrumental songs are good, but they may speak more to you than to God. Play them as background music while you read the Bible.

- If you need to, print out the lyrics and make a basic song book. You can find lyrics to most songs with the right Google search (e.g., *I Can Only Imagine* lyrics).

- A worship song is a good way to get things started. One song may be enough, and you still have other ways (STONES) to worship. (And… you may need to get to school or work. Don't be late.) Remember you are worshiping all day long. (We'll get to that more in chapter 13.)

- You may not need the music to sing in worship to God. Remember my go-to song? "I love you Lord, and I lift my voice." I just sing it and it seems to put me in the right frame of mind. Find a good go-to song that speaks to you and God (or use mine). You're welcome.

- Don't worry about singing the whole song or knowing the words perfectly. Just let the artists sing their song, through your heart. Listen to their words, and just let them be yours. That's the whole point of worship songs. You let the writer put words and melody in your mouth, your mind, and your heart that you want to say or sing to God. The chorus alone might be enough. Maybe that's the part you remember and can sing back to God on your own.

- This is not screen time. Have some discipline, and stay away from social media or email, for heaven's sake. If you use your phone for your music, turn it off after the song. *Off,* not silent.

- Remember: you are worshiping God! Don't let anything distract you from that. If the technology is a distraction or is too much to deal with, then hand-write some choruses from a hymnal in a spiral notebook or in the back pages of your prayer journal. Keep them with your Bible and forget about everything else.

- Sing to God. He loves it when you sing to Him.

10

THE PSALMS IN WORSHIP

I grew up in the Methodist church. I mean that literally. We lived out in the country and went to a country church, Eliam United Methodist, in the small community of Fortsonia in Elbert County in northeast Georgia. Every time the church doors were open, we were there! Lots of those times, it was Daddy who unlocked the door. We were faithful Methodists. I don't mean to make light of this commitment.

> *Enter His gates with thanksgiving And His courts with praise. Give thanks to Him, bless His name. For the Lord is good; His lovingkindness is everlasting. And His faithfulness to all generations.*
>
> – MOSES BEN AMRAM (Ps. 100:4, NASB)

Looking back, it was such a privilege to grow up in a loving Christian home where we went to church regularly. That's just what we did; there was never any discussion or decision to make. I raised my family with the same understanding about church. We are no longer Methodists but, still, it's just what we do. We go to church.

As Methodists, we got a brand-new preacher every four years whether we needed one or not. This is just how the Methodist Church works. We shared our circuit preacher with three other tiny Methodist congregations in the rural area called Flatwoods.

On Sunday mornings at Eliam, we all sat as a family in the same pew every week. Mama sang in the choir with about a dozen other good-hearted souls. They all sang the same melody part, roughly, and led our congregation of 70-or-so in the good old-timey hymns. We sang from a little brown book called the *Cokesbury Worship Hymnal*. Not an inch thick, it still held all the traditional hymns of Charles Wesley, Fanny Crosby, and Isaac Watts. I have one open in front of me as I write.

In the church sanctuary, we had a small ornately framed placard that hung on the wall over the piano where everyone could see it. It simply said "HYMNS" at the top, and down below were the slide-in numbers of the hymns for that Sunday's worship service. Every Sunday, the choir leader, a tremendously tall man named Mr. Dye, stood up and called us to our feet. "Turn over in your hymn books to number 76, *Rock of Ages Cleft for Me*." We opened up our Cokesbury and sang all three hymns shown on the placard, first, second, and last stanzas. Before the sermon, we sang *The Doxology*:

> Praise God, from whom all blessings flow.
> Praise Him, all creatures here below.
> Praise Him above, ye heavenly host.
> Praise Father, Son, and Holy Ghost. Aaaaaaameennn.[44]

Mama lived to be 92. I spoke at her funeral there at Eliam, just five years ago. We sang from the *Cokesbury Hymnal* the songs she had picked out for us.

The book of Psalms is the Hebrew hymnal. Of the 150 "songs," about half are attributed to King David who, as we know, was a musician from his early years. The others have various authors like Asaph, the sons of Korah, Solomon, and even ones by (or perhaps for) Moses. Authorship of the Psalms is kind of fuzzy at best. The Psalms reveal the very soul of the nation of Israel, as well as the trials, sins, and worship of King David himself. They span a period of 500 years of Hebrew history. Psalms were associated primarily with temple worship in Jerusalem. They were sung with music or even used as liturgies, read aloud, or spoken in unison by a worshiping congregation.

If there is one primal theme that permeates the Psalms, it's praise for YHWH. The name "YHWH" appears more than 750 times in the 150 Psalms. The Psalms lead worshipers in the worship of our God, then and now.

Take a quick look at YHWH in the Psalms in the Appendix. It will give you a list of things that the Psalms say about YHWH and instructions for us in our worship of Him. Here are a few.

- Praise YHWH
- Hope in YHWH
- YHWH, my refuge and my fortress
- Great is YHWH and greatly to be praised

The Psalms exist to help us worship YHWH. You can use them in any way that suits you. Just pick one and read it to God as if it were your own words. Find a passage you like and make it your own. Write it down or, better yet, memorize it and just speak it to God. Let's practice that.

> "I love you, LORD; you are my strength. The LORD is my rock, my fortress, and my savior; my God is my rock, in whom I find protection. He is my shield, the power that saves me, and my place of safety. I called on the LORD, who is worthy of praise, and he saved me from my enemies." (Psalm 18:1–3, NLT)

Now, learn to replace "LORD" and "The LORD" with "Yahweh." If you like, you can replace "God" with "Elohim" (el-o-heem´).

> "I love you, Yahweh; you are my strength. Yahweh is my rock, my fortress, and my savior; my Elohim is my rock, in whom I find protection. He is my shield, the power that saves me, and my place of safety. I called on Yahweh, who is worthy of praise…" (Psalm 18:1–3, NLT Author's translation added)

You can even replace the names and pronouns of God with a personal pronoun. Make the passage and the praise your own, and speak it to God as if you wrote it for Him.

> "I love You, Yahweh; You are my strength. <u>You</u> are my rock, my fortress, and my savior; <u>You</u> are my rock, in whom I find protection. <u>You</u> are my shield, the power that saves me, and my place of safety. I am calling on <u>You</u>, Yahweh, <u>You</u> are worthy of praise…" (Psalm 18:1–3 Author's translation)

The Psalms provide a primary worship tool from the Bible. Learn to use them in your daily altar.

At the same time, the Psalms are scripture, God-breathed, which qualifies them to give an authentic view of God's character and His requirements.

> "I waited patiently for the LORD; And He inclined to me and heard my cry. He brought me up out of the pit of destruction, out of the miry clay, And He set my feet upon a rock making my footsteps firm. He put a new song in my mouth, a song of praise to our God; Many will see and fear and will trust in the LORD." (Psalm 40:1–3, NASB95)

David expresses personal experience with YHWH. Have you ever felt like your feet were stuck in the miry mud of life? Are you always looking up out of a hole you have dug for yourself? Maybe a financial pit, or a sin pit, or a relationship pit? David said He "waited patiently for YHWH." He knew YHWH was there, waiting for him to cry out from the quicksand. He remembered how YHWH leaned over and heard his cry, like a father would lean down to his child. God brought David out and set his feet on solid ground. He gave David a new song to sing, a song of worship to Elohim. People would see David's deliverance and put their trust in YHWH.

What a story! And just because it might be written in some sort of prose or verse, that makes it all the better. You can believe that our God is that kind of God. A Father who will let His son or daughter make mistakes they can learn from. That's tough love. But He is never far away, always ready to lift us up and brush us off. Always willing to remind us that He is there if we will just trust Him enough to cry out to Him.

I want to worship a father like that one!

The great hymn writer, Isaac Watts, once wrote that the Psalms were:

> "confessions of sins you never committed, with complaints of sorrows which you never felt; cursing such enemies as you never had, and thanksgiving for such victories as you never obtained; leading you to speak of things, places, and actions you never knew."

As you read the book of Psalms, you may feel, at times, the same distant way as Mr. Watts. But look at David's sorrows as your own (Psalm 40). Consider carefully who your "enemies" are (Psalm 54). David's repentance may begin to sound a lot like your repentant heart (Psalm 51). Celebrate David's victories as your own (Psalm 62).

> "As the deer pants for the water brooks, So my soul pants for You, O God. My soul thirsts for God, for the living God; When shall I come and appear before God?" (Psalm 42:1-2, NASB95)

> "Why are you in despair, O my soul? And why have you become disturbed within me? Hope in God, for I shall again praise Him For the help of His presence. O my God, my soul is in despair within me..." (Psalm 42:5-6a, NASB95)

GREG DIXON

The Psalms express every emotion. Sadness – lament – joy – victory – remorse – despair – anger – hope.

Pray the Psalms. Own the Psalms. YHWH wrote them for you.

Come, O come, let us worship
Sing unto the Lord with thanksgiving.
O come, O come, let us worship
Sing unto the Lord with thanksgiving.[45]

Cokesbury Worship Hymnal, Hymn 295 (Psalm 95:6 & Psalm 147:7)
By May F. Lawrence. Copyright Lamar & Whitman.

11

WORSHIP AS WARFARE

I sin. I'm a Spirit-filled, blood-bought believer in Jesus Christ, yet I sin. I do. Nothing disappoints me more than when I disappoint my Father. I also suffer through times of trials and difficulties; how I respond tests my character, resolve, and dependence on Holy Spirit who endures, exhorts, and encourages

> *When your spirit is heavy, when your heart is broken, when your burdens seem unbearable – trust Him. Look to Him.*
>
> — ANNE GRAHAM LOTZ

me all the way. In this chapter I want to deal with temptation, trials, and suffering and demonstrate how worship is our greatest weapon in these spiritual battles.

Worship in Times of Temptation

My earthly father's name was Paul. His friends called him "Pete," but we just called him "Daddy." He was a veteran of World War II and fought the Japanese for two years in the Aleutian Island chain off the coast of Alaska. During this conflict, the Japanese would take an island, and the Americans would take it back. It became a war of attrition that the American infantryman and airman finally won by having more wins than losses. The Aleutian theater marked the closest that Japan ever got to the American mainland. Now, in hindsight, we know we won that battle and the war; but in 1942 and 43, it was a bloody, day-by-day battle for what was right and sacred. For freedom and democracy.

Daddy was a good man with a strong faith, quiet and firm in his daily walk. He rarely ever talked about those war years. We begged him for stories, but he just couldn't go there again. The memories stayed locked up inside him.

I know He loved me; he showed it in a thousand ways. But he was sparse with a compliment or word of encouragement. If I made a good play at third base, he was quiet about it. My mother might shout "Good play, Gregory!" but not Daddy. You practiced hard to make good plays like that one! You put your head down and plowed through. That's just what you did. So, I practiced hard.

I worked hard for his approval. Growing up, the one thing I most wanted was just to please my Daddy; I hated to displease him. When I did something wrong, his quiet sideways look with a little shake of his head devastated me. It crushed me. Yeah, I might get some punishment for failing to finish his assigned task or leaving his tools out in the rain. But his silent disapproval felt worse than his punishment. I can feel it right now in the pit of my stomach.

He's been gone for many years, but I still love and miss him. He is still my life hero. And I am proud to say I'm a lot like him.

To this day, in the same way I felt about my daddy, I still hate to disappoint my Abba. When I fail Him and sin, I can "see" the small shake of His head. I can feel His disappointment in the pit of my stomach. The Bible calls this "conviction of sin," and Holy Spirit inside me is "grieved" by my sin. It's His grief I feel in the pit of my stomach.

I know He loves me; He has shown it in a thousand ways. I know He will discipline me, which always reminds me I am truly His child. But it still hurts. I hate to disappoint Him. So, I practice hard, and worship is my best strategy toward pleasing Abba. Let me explain.

I am at war with my flesh. It's a lot like the battle for the Aleutians. Back and forth, day by day, a fight for what is right and sacred. And the older I get, my win/loss ratio improves. I guess I shouldn't feel too badly about this daily warfare since I'm in pretty good company with another fellow named Paul.

"For we know that the Law is spiritual, but I am of flesh, sold into bondage to sin. For what I am doing, I do not understand; for I am not practicing what I would like to do, but I am doing the very thing I hate. But if I do the very thing I do not want to do, I agree with the Law, confessing that the Law is good. So now, no longer am I the one doing it, but sin which dwells in me. For I know that nothing good dwells in me, that is, in my flesh; for the willing is present in me, but the doing of the good is not. For the good that I want, I do not do, but I practice the very evil that I do not want. But if I am doing the very thing I do not want, I am no longer the one doing it, but sin which dwells in me. I find then the principle that evil is present in me, the one who wants to do good. For I joyfully concur with the law of God in the inner man, but I see a different law in the members of my body, waging war against the law of my mind and making me a prisoner of the law of sin which is in my members. Wretched man that I am! Who will set me free from the body of this death?" (Romans 7:14–24, NASB95)

The Apostle Paul, it seems, was at war with his own flesh as well. The law of Christ in his mind said one thing, and the law in his flesh said another. He was amazingly transparent about the whole thing. He states three times in these verses that he wants to do good; then, he states four times that he is doing what is wrong in God's eyes. Finally, he states five times that the cause of this constant battle is the sin which dwells in him. Sin dwells right alongside Holy Spirit, who also dwells inside him.

Oh boy! Do I relate!

So, what can we do about this war with sin? Maybe we should just accept it as part of life. "I'm going to sin, I'm forgiven, and God is gracious, so what's the problem?" To that, Paul says, "No WAY!"

"What shall we say then? Are we to continue in sin so that grace may increase? May it never be! How shall we who died to sin still live in it?" (Romans 6:1–2, NASB95)

What can we do? *We can fight!*

"Finally, be strong in the Lord and in the strength of His might. Put on the full armor of God, so that you will be able to stand firm against the schemes of the devil. For our struggle is not against flesh and blood, but against the rulers, against the powers, against the world forces of this darkness, against the spiritual forces of wickedness in the heavenly places.

"Therefore, take up the full armor of God, so that you will be able to resist in the evil day, and having done everything, to stand firm. Stand firm therefore, HAVING GIRDED YOUR LOINS WITH TRUTH, and HAVING PUT ON THE BREASTPLATE OF RIGHTEOUSNESS, and having shod YOUR FEET WITH THE PREPARATION OF THE GOSPEL OF PEACE; in addition to all, taking up the shield of faith with which you will be able to extinguish all the flaming arrows of the evil one. And take THE HELMET OF SALVATION, and the sword of the Spirit, which is the word of God. With all prayer and petition pray at all times in the Spirit, and with this in view, be on the alert with all perseverance and petition for all the saints..." (Ephesians 6:10–18, NASB95)

This powerful passage provides the classic scriptural approach to waging war against temptation, sin, and Satan himself. You should begin your warfare against temptation and sin here in Ephesians 6 by putting on the full armor of God.

In my battle against sin, worship is my biggest ally, my secret weapon. If you are tempted to sin, go to God. In fact, *race* to God! But don't start with, "And do not lead us into temptation, but deliver us from evil." (Matthew 6:13, NASB95)

Start out by BLESSING God and THANKING Him that He is THERE for you. PRAISE Him for His faithfulness and lovingkindness. THANK Him mostly for His "once-and-for-all forgiveness."

Talk to Jesus about your temptation. He understands.

> "Therefore, since we have a great high priest who has passed through the heavens, Jesus the Son of God, let us hold fast our confession." (Hebrews 4:14, NASB95)

Remember the role of the high priest in temple worship. He stood *before* God and *between* God and the people, the mediator who made the animal sacrifice to pay for the people's sins. Our high priest is Jesus, the Son of God. Wow!! He made the ultimate blood sacrifice for us and now sits at the Father's right hand, ever making intercession for you and me.

> "For we do not have a high priest who cannot sympathize with our weaknesses, but One who has been tempted in all things as we are, yet without sin." (Hebrews 4:15, NASB95)

Remember, our high priest was tempted with the same things we are most vulnerable to and, yet, He resisted the devil's efforts to make Him sin (Matt. 4).

> "Therefore, let us draw near with confidence to the throne of grace, so that we may receive mercy and find grace to help in time of need." (Hebrews 4:16, NASB95)

I love the word, "Therefore." Since all these things about Jesus are true, (therefore) you can draw near (in worship) to the throne of grace, with confidence, that you will receive mercy and find grace just when you need them most. Every Christian can!

But… what if I've already sinned? I flunked the temptation test, and now I've done it again.

Well, the end is the same, but the beginning is different. Just go before God in a solemn, sincere PRAYER and CONFESS the sin. Spell it out and don't mince words. Express your regret and sorrow. (Say, "I am sorry.") Your forgiveness is already in place, so you don't need to beg for something you already have.

Next, express your plan of REPENTANCE. What have you done or what will you do to reverse course and get back on track? Just tell your Abba how you will correct this sinful behavior.

(If you are not really sorry you sinned, then I might suggest you reconsider your salvation. Saved people have Holy Spirit, and Holy Spirit grieves over every sin. Just sayin'…)

Once you've confessed and repented, you have to move past this. God is faithful to do His part. Trust me in this: I have lots of first-hand knowledge.

> "If we confess our sins, He is faithful and righteous to forgive us our sins and to cleanse us from all unrighteousness." (1 John 1:9, NASB95)

Now go to Him in worship. Just go, without saying "Amen." You are closest to ABBA and ABBA is closest to you in these times of transparency and dependence. Think about it for a minute: when are you least likely to give in to temptation? When you are worshiping ABBA, right? No little kid would color on the wall with his parent right there watching. You are safe now in His PRESENCE, with CLEAN HANDS and a PURE HEART. So, REST in this time of worship. REST from your flesh and temptations and struggles with the world. Know that Abba loves you, will comfort you, and reassure you that you belong to Him.

The more I worship, the less I sin. My worship experience carries over as I move on to what's next in my day. I feel His presence linger the way I do after I kiss Vicki. I can still taste her and smell her. I feel her close to me, even after we have gone our separate ways. It's the same when I worship my Abba. I feel DELIGHT and JOY and PEACE and safety, and I find CONFIDENCE and strength to "Get back in the ballgame, Boy. You got this."

Worship can be your secret weapon, too. But like any weapon, you have to remember to keep it loaded and clean. It has to be nearby. It has to be familiar. You must practice with it. This way, when you need your weapon, it's a natural thing to reach for it, and Boom! God is there. The battle is won!

Worship in Times of Testing and Suffering

Testing and temptation have a lot in common. But don't confuse the two. God will never tempt us, but He *will* test us. Much of what you just learned about temptation and sin can be applied here as well.

Suffering can also test us. Suffering comes in lost relationships, from health concerns, from trauma, from loneliness, and so much more. The Covid 19 pandemic contributed to all these areas of suffering for people all over the world. Christians suffered as much as any others. We lost loved ones, we suffered with the disease itself and, perhaps, most common of all we suffered loneliness and isolation. We couldn't attend church. People who lived by themselves were stuck at home, alone with their fears and the four walls. Seniors were sequestered in nursing homes without visits from family. Kids were away from their friends in school and the socialization they need.

Suffering is the everyday life condition of so many people in our world. But suffering was the plight of our Savior as well. James and Paul both exhorted us to *rejoice* in our sufferings. It's our *response* to suffering that God most wants to see! Our response can and should bring Him glory. So, suffering surely is a test of our relationship with the Father.

Let's roll up tests, trials, and suffering under one word: *tests*. Tests can come from any of several sources.

Tests can come from the world. Maybe your work, your finances, or your relationships with others generate tests for you. Maybe you have an ethical dilemma at work or a shortfall in funds to pay your bills. Maybe your job is just too stressful, and things have come to a head with your boss. (I'm relating some of the trials I have endured in my work and personal life.) These stressors are common to us all at one time or another.

Tests can come from family. Especially teenagers. If you have raised children, I need say no more. At times we face prolonged trials with our spouse. Relationships can sour, and it seems we can do nothing to make them work the way they did before. Difficulties can arise with family members and bring a downward spiral that seems impossible to fix.

Tests can come from our bodies. Handling health concerns can be a major test of our faith and character. Our health or family members' health can be some of the most common and difficult trials we can face. They are almost inevitable.

Tests can come from Satan. The devil wants nothing more than to separate us from our heavenly father, and tests of our faith are his favorite tactic. (Sometimes it's hard to tell whether Satan is behind the test or if it's from one of the other sources I've already mentioned.) Satan's tests are usually diabolical in nature and hard to figure out the source.

Tests can come from God. Our Father will test us from time to time, usually to teach us a critical life lesson or discipline us for disobedience. Or He may just design His tests to see His own glory in us and in our response to the circumstance! Like any father, God wants us to grow up and be a mature, contributing member of society. He wants to mold us into the likeness of Jesus.

> "Consider it all joy, my brethren, when you encounter various trials, knowing that the testing of your faith produces endurance. And let endurance have its perfect result, so that you may be perfect and complete, lacking in nothing." (James 1:2–4, NASB95)

James starts with "*when* you encounter various trials." He knows they *will* happen and come from various sources. His prescription for success is endurance. Sometimes that's all we can do, just put our heads down and pray/plow our way through it. Prayer is certainly our first and best approach when we encounter various trials. Trials are integral parts of God's work in our lives and can display His power and glory in us.[23]

Let's think about what we've already learned about worship as a weapon. Our trials (and temptations) demand a response on our part. They can get the best of us if we are not armed and ready for them. Worship is certainly one of our best weapons in these times.

Worship the Father and thank Him for the trials you are encountering. BLESS God and THANK Him that He is THERE for you! PRAISE Him for His faithfulness and discipline. Be JOYFUL, knowing that these trials will have a positive outcome in your life. *Put your head down and worship your way through the trials of life.*

In his book, *Peaks and Pits*, Roger Mardis says it best.

> "Our worship is always crucial but especially in moments of hardship and seasons of trouble. Why? Because worship is a transfer of focus; it is a shifting of one's attention. In worship, my focus is no longer on myself or my situation; it's on my Lord. In this way, my worry can become worship, my pain can become praise, and my agony can result in adoration. Worship is not just a weekly service we attend; it is a daily practice of a growing and hurting believer." (Mardis 2020)[24]

There's a sling in my voice and a stone in my praise
Pushing back when the darkest weapons form
There's a power on my lips even death can't defy
When the name of our God is lifted high
'Cause there is resurrection power
When we sing the name of Jesus
Resurrection power
When we raise a mighty sound.[48]

> *When we worship, we pull armies from another realm into battle.*
>
> – BRIAN JOHNSON BETHEL MUSIC

Brian Johnson, Chris Davenport, Bethel Music

For further study see the website – http://www.priorityofworship.com

12

WHOM WE WORSHIP

This may sound like an obvious question, but work with me for a little while. We talked about worshiping other "gods." So, we know what *not* to worship. We've spent most of this book learning how to worship the One True God,

> *To worship in spirit is to draw near to God with an undivided heart.*
>
> – ERWIN LUTZER

YHWH. We've learned who He is and discovered some of His many wonderful qualities that make Him worthy of our worship. So, yeah, we worship YHWH, God the Father.

I dare say it would take a million Bibles to explain fully and reveal completely our God. We understand that we can only know God as He has chosen to reveal Himself to us. We are reminded in Hebrews:

> "In the past God spoke to our forefathers through the prophets at many times and in various ways, but in these last days he has spoken to us by his Son, whom he appointed heir of all things, and through whom he made the universe. The Son is the radiance of God's glory and the exact representation of his being, sustaining all things by his powerful word. After he had provided purification for sins, he sat down at the right hand of the Majesty in heaven." (Hebrews 1:1–3, NIV84)

Jesus Christ, Yeshua Hamashiach, perfectly represents God in the flesh. He was and is our example for living.

> "He said to them, 'But who do you say that I am?' Simon Peter answered, 'You are the Christ, the Son of the living God.'" (Matthew 16:15–16, NASB95)

We could go on and on about our Jesus, but I am reminded of two simple statements He made about Himself and His deity.

"Truly, truly, I say to you, before Abraham was born, I am." (John 8:58, NASB95)
"I and the Father are one." (John 10:30, NASB95)

So yes. We should also worship Jesus directly and freely. Speak to Him by name when you worship. Call Him Jesus, call Him Yeshua. Call Him…

Master, Savior, Lion of Judah
Blessed Prince of Peace
Shepherd, Fortress, Rock of Salvation, Lamb of God is He
Son of David, King of the Ages, Eternal Life
Holy Lord of Glory, His name is Life.[47]

He is our pattern for how to love the Father and love others. He is our ransom, our redeemer, our righteousness. He is our savior. Every quality that is true of God the Father is true of God the Son.

Worship Jesus.

Holy Spirit is the third person of the Trinity.

YHWH is called a "Triune God." Tri = 3, une = is unity. Three in One.

- We see Him manifested as God the Father.
- We see Him manifested as God the Son.
- We see Him manifested as God the Holy Spirit.

Collectively, we might refer to the Trinity as "The Godhead."

Nowhere in the Bible do we ever see the word "trinity," or "triune," or "Godhead" for that matter. But we do *see* "the Trinity," the Triune God, because the whole Bible is about this Triune God.

Primarily in the Old Testament we see God as *God the Father.* YHWH related to mankind predominantly through a special nation, a chosen people.

Then, at the beginning of the New Testament, we see God as *God the Son.* Jesus related to mankind primarily through the church. (Believers.)

After Pentecost in the New Testament, we see God as *God the Holy Spirit.* Holy Spirit relates (present tense) to mankind on an individual level, one person at a time.

You may have noticed in my writing that I rarely refer to Holy Spirit as "The" Holy Spirit. I see Him as a person, in the same sense that I see YHWH and Jesus. I would never write about "The" Jesus. Holy Spirit is one of the three "persons" of the trinity. If you are uncomfortable with this designation, you can refer to Him as The Holy Spirit if you like. That is certainly the traditional way and biblical model.

Holy Spirit is the "vicar" of Christ. (The one and only Vicar of Christ.[25]) A vicar is a representative or surrogate for one more superior. Think of the word "vicarious." Holy Spirit vicariously brings the presence and power of the resurrected Jesus into the lives of individual believers and into the Church at large. Just before His ascension, in Matthew 28, Jesus issued the Great Commission for His followers, present and future, to go and make disciples. He ends the commission with these words:

> … And surely I am with you always, to the very end of the age."
> (Matthew 28:20 NIV84)

"I am with you always…" How could this be true if He was going back to His Father?

> "I will ask the Father, and He will give you another Helper (PARACLETE), that He may be with you forever; that is the Spirit of truth, whom the world cannot receive, because it does not see Him or know Him, but you know Him because He abides with you and will be in you. I will not leave you as orphans; I will come to you." (John 14:16-18 NASB95 Author's translation added)

PARACLETE is translated variously as Helper (NASB95), Counselor (NIV84), and Advocate (NLT). Literally it means "one who comes alongside; called to one's aid." Through the Paraclete, Jesus is present and involved in every believer. Another Helper, Counselor, Advocate, like Jesus. Abiding, remaining with you and in you. Holy Spirit is Jesus in us.

As Holy Spirit became more prevalent in the New Testament, He filled Jesus, He filled the Apostles, and He filled every new believer. But is Holy Spirit found in the Old Testament? You bet! But you have to pay attention to find Him.

Many of the times you see God actively going forth to empower someone, equip someone, prophesy through someone, or do a supernatural act, God the Holy Spirit is in action. Both the Old Testament and the New Testament are full of these occurrences.

Yahweh is not a physical being. He is a Spirit by nature. His Spirit is distinct from all other spiritual beings in that He is Holy, perfectly unique. However, humans have trouble describing or relating to a spiritual being. So, when we write about them, we tend to use words that we can relate to. Both in the Old Testament and the New, writers described Holy Spirit as "wind" or "breath." You can't see the wind, but it is real, and has an effect on its surroundings.

In the Old Testament we see God the Holy Spirit called the "RUACH" (or RUAH) which is Hebrew for "breath."

> "In the beginning God created the heavens and the earth. The earth was formless and void, and darkness was over the surface of the deep, and the <u>Spirit of God</u> was moving over the surface of the waters." (Genesis 1:1–2, NASB95)

The Spirit of God, the "RUACH of Elohim," was the "Breath of God" at work in creating the world.

In the New Testament, we see God's Spirit in Acts 2:

> "When the day of Pentecost came, they were all together in one place. Suddenly a sound like the <u>blowing of a violent wind</u> came from heaven and filled the whole house where they were sitting. They saw what seemed to be tongues of fire that separated and came to rest on each of them. All of them were <u>filled with the Holy Spirit</u> and began to speak in other tongues as the Spirit enabled them." (Acts 2:1–4, NIV84)

We also see Holy Spirit in many other new ways. In Greek, the words we translate as Holy Spirit are "HAGIOS PNEUMA" (silent P). HAGIOS = Holy. PNEUMA = Spirit. Does the word "pneuma" look familiar? A "pneumatic" tire is filled with air; a "pneumatic" drill is powered by air.

Where else do we see the breath of God in action?

"THEOS PNEUMA" (or THEÓPNEUSTOS). All scripture is "God breathed" (2 Timothy 3:16, NIV84).

Throughout the New Testament, God the Holy Spirit goes forth from God the Father to accomplish His will in a person, an individual.

If His will is to *save* someone, then Holy Spirit *draws* that person to respond to the gospel. If His will is to *empower* someone, then Holy Spirit works in the life of that believer to give them power.

Every true believer and follower of Christ has *God the Holy Spirit* living inside of them. Every day. Hagios Pneuma lives inside of every follower of Jesus. In fact, there can be no such thing as a "saved person" without Holy Spirit. Essential to the Christian life, Holy Spirit gives us power to witness and pray, He assures us of our salvation, and He convicts us of sin. When we open our Bibles, He is our teacher. He is the author who sits right there beside us as we read His book. God the Holy Spirit relates to mankind on an individual basis.

> "In the same way the Spirit also helps our weakness; for we do not know how to pray as we should, but the Spirit Himself intercedes for us with groanings too deep for words; and He who searches the hearts knows what the mind of the Spirit is, because He intercedes for the saints according to the will of God." (Romans 8:26–27, NASB95)

When we pray or worship, Holy Spirit "helps our weakness." He speaks to Jesus on our behalf in a way that goes beyond any words we might have. God the Spirit speaks to God the Son, according to the will of God the Father, so we can pray and worship effectively.

With the help of the Holy Spirit, we will worship The Father through Jesus.

Should we worship Holy Spirit? *Absolutely!*
Directly and by name.

When you worship YHWH or Jesus, you may picture them in heaven on a throne. Somewhere out there. You may want to reach out to them, like a child reaches out to her daddy. We may raise our hands or put them out with our palms open and upward, as though we are giving or receiving something. All this is good and appropriate if you find some joy or meaning in these actions.

But let me challenge you to do something different: when you worship Holy Spirit, He is not "out there someplace." He is right here inside you. So, you might just put one hand or both on your chest or wrap your arms around yourself. At times, I might open the middle button on my shirt, and slip my right hand inside, just over my heart. When I do this, I promise I can feel His warmth, His presence. In church, while others have their hands raised, I have mine on myself in a way that touches Holy Spirit within me. I speak to Him directly and thank Him for teaching me, convicting me, helping me, encouraging me, and for never leaving me alone. I praise Holy Spirit just as I would praise YHWH or Yeshua.

They are all God. All holy and worthy of my worship. Together and individually.
So, whom do I worship?
I worship YHWH, my Abba, my provider, and my shepherd.
I worship Jesus, my savior, my truth, and my friend.
I worship Holy Spirit, my encourager, my helper, and my teacher.

> And the church of Christ was born, then the Spirit lit the flame
> Now this gospel truth of old shall not kneel, shall not faint
> By His blood and in His name, in His freedom I am free
> For the love of Jesus Christ Who has resurrected me
> Praise the Father, praise the Son
> Praise the Spirit, three in one
> God of glory, Majesty
> Praise forever to the King of Kings.[50]

King of Kings - Hillsong Worship

13

WHEN TO WORSHIP

Worship has a rhythm. That's the way God designed it.

"Remember the sabbath day, to keep it holy. For in six days the LORD made the heavens and the earth, the sea and all that is in them, and rested on the seventh day; therefore, the LORD blessed the sabbath day and made it holy." (Exodus 20:8, 11, NASB95)

"Sabbath" *(or SHABBAT)* means "rest." One day in seven is set aside when we don't do our regular work but instead do other things like rest, worship, and enjoy family time. The Jews designated their sabbath as the hours from Friday at sundown to Saturday at sundown.

> *Worship is the way of life for those entranced by and passionate for the glory of God.*
>
> – MATT CHANDLER

Christians moved our sabbath to Sunday, the day that Jesus was raised up from the grave, "the Lord's Day." So traditionally, Sunday is the day we all gather for church. I don't want to make too much of this point, but God never said, "You shall worship on the sabbath." He just said to keep it holy, separated, and special from the other days of the week. But there is wisdom in designating Sunday as a day of rest and worship. It breaks up the seven-day cycle for us. Things can "start over" on Monday morning with a fresh, new beginning.

Cycles and rhythms are important to humans. The rhythm of sun-up and sun-down gives us a cycle for work, home, and sleep. The truth is that our health and well-being depend on these cycles. I need to exercise, but I don't like to. The best way for me to exercise regularly is to set a time each day, early in the day, to go to the YMCA. It's just what I do (remember, I'm retired). If I say, "Well, I'll go to the Y sometime most every day," then I don't go to the Y *any* day. I'm lazy like that. But, with a set time and a rhythm in my life, things get done.

And so it is with worship.

We should designate a day of the week for rest and "family" worship. Of course, the world still turns on Sunday, and people have to work. I get that. People who don't work on Sundays should respect and support those who do, and those who do work on Sundays should designate a different day as their sabbath. Having a regular day that includes an hour or more of worship is important and even better if you can do it with other Christians. "Church" may be a weekly event with you and your family.

But worship is not a weekly event. *It cannot be!*

Worship is a posture for everyday living. An everyday attitude that honors God through obedience to His will and acknowledgment of His worth. Your worship is personal; it looks like you; it sounds like you; and it pleases God all the more when it comes from your heart (not directly from a how-to book).

Start your day with quiet time and start your quiet time with worship. Read, then pray, but don't say "Amen." Amen means "may it be so." Leave your prayer channel open…all day.

Then, live out the rest of your day in an attitude of worship and prayer. Just speak to God continually as if He were in the front seat beside you, walking along with you, standing close by, sitting at your table, in the next cubicle. God can hear your thoughts, but I believe He likes to hear your words.

He is there to listen to your concerns, clear your mind, check your attitude, encourage you, direct you, convict you, and empower you. He is also there to hear your praise and accept your thanks. To enjoy your song, receive your acknowledgements of His character, be proud

> *Work becomes worship when you dedicate it to God and perform it with an awareness of His presence.*
> – RICK WARREN

of your obedience, and be glorified by your walking in a manner worthy of your calling as His child. He can hear your faintest praise, your unspoken thanks, your thoughts of Him, and see your smile meant just for Him. He is always with you. Jesus promised us this.

> "I will ask the Father, and He will give you another Helper, that He may be with you forever; that is the Spirit of truth, whom the world cannot receive, because it does not see Him or know Him, but you know Him because He abides with you and will be in you." (John 14:16–17, NASB95)

When you lay down at night to sleep, *then* you can say "Amen" to that day. "Abba, may it be so."

When you worship, remember: God is Elohim, the Father, your Creator. God is also Yeshua, the Son, your Savior. God is also Holy Spirit, the Breath of Life, and your Helper. The Father and The Son are in Heaven. Holy Spirit lives inside you. So, in reality, God is closer than the front seat or within arm's reach. Holy Spirit hears every word you speak and every thought you think 24/7. He sees everything you look at and feels your deepest feelings. He abides. That means He remains in you and with you, even when you sin, even when you ignore Him. He keeps you connected to God, even when you grieve Him with your disobedience. He loves you that much.

As you worship throughout your day, picture God, not as "out there" somewhere or even just over there close by, but right *in here*. Place your hand on your chest and you can feel His presence. God lives within you, just as He did in the Old Testament temple. He no longer dwells, hidden behind the veil in the Holy of Holies. The veil was torn in two at the cross and removed forever. The New Testament temple is you. Right there inside your body.

> "Or do you not know that your body is a temple of the Holy Spirit who is in you, whom you have from God, and that you are not your own? For you have been bought with a price: therefore, glorify God in your body." (1 Corinthians 6:19–20, NASB95)

Just as the priests cared for the temple of cloth or stone, you should care for your own temple. A priest might have swept the floor or cleaned the ashes from the altar as his acts of worship. These everyday actions proved his obedience and devotion to YHWH. So, what are your acts of obedience and devotion in *your* temple? Our lives can be filled with too much and too little. Too much food or screen time or recreation. Too little rest or exercise or consideration of others. Your temple is very expensive, purchased at great price by God, so He has a right to expect you to take good care of it. How you live your life day-by-day and moment-by-moment is a critical part of how you worship.

When you look into the refrigerator or at a menu, think of Him, your SUFFICIENCY. When you plan your day, think of Him, your BANNER. When you sit down at night or decide what to watch on TV, think of Him, your SANCTIFIER. When you look at social media, think of Him, your SHEPHERD. When you lay down and close your eyes to sleep, think of Him, your ABBA.

Worship God every day, all day long.

Quiet Time

OK let's drill down a bit more into the ordering of your day.
What is a quiet time?

- My quiet time is when I spend *quality* time with God.
- My quiet time is where I build my *relationship* with God.
- My quiet time is a two-way *conversation* with God that improves over time.
- It's called a "quiet" time because *distractions* slow my spiritual progress.

If you are married right now, then you know the value of "date night." (Husbands, if you don't, then there are some other "how-to" books you need to read like *Marriage for Dummies*.) Having a regular date night is essential for a healthy marriage, especially in the first two or three decades. After that, it's even more important. (I've been married to Vicki for 44 years and counting.) But I digress. To have a date night you must plan for date night. You get a babysitter if needed. You set aside time. You dress up some. You guys open the car door for your wives, right? Ladies, you might be like Vicki who puts on lipstick and hands the tube to your husband to put in his pocket. You go out to a restaurant, leave your children at home and your phones in the car. You talk. You catch up. You plan. You laugh. Maybe you drink a glass of wine. Or not. Maybe you go to a movie. Or maybe you go home and snuggle. Date night is important. Date night is where you build your relationship. It's quality time. No distractions. Good two-way conversation. Planning. Dreaming.

But is date night *the only time* you build relationship with your wife or husband? No. You build relationship every day. If you *only* build relationship on date nights, your relationship will struggle over time. Relationship, whether it be with your spouse or with God, *must be daily,* at the very least.

In our relationship with God, date night might be like church on Sunday. We plan for it. It's good to worship, pray, sing, and read the Bible with other believers and our family members. But if church on Sunday is the only time you worship or pray or read the Bible, then your relationship with God will falter over time.

Quiet time is our *everyday quality and quantity* time with God.

Good quiet times with God will routinely contain these three elements: *worship, the Bible, and prayer.* They may contain other things like study, writing, thinking, and listening. But think of the basis for any quiet time as worship, Bible, and prayer. I find that my QT is incomplete without all three. (Of course, this is just my humble opinion, but I'm writing the book.)

Let me talk about prayer first, even though it might be the way you end your QT. Keep it simple. When you pray...

- Always *be aware* of who God is and what He has done for you. Don't just ask for stuff.
- *Be honest* with God. Admit your sins and make plans to correct them.
- *Approach* God like a child would approach a loving father. Talk to Him about yourself and others. Ask Him questions. Just talk, and don't worry about form or language or anything complicated.
- Just tell Him your thoughts. *He's listening.*

As for the Bible, just read it. As you read, ask yourself simple questions that are meaningful to you...

- What does it say?
- What does it mean?
- What does it mean to me?
- What did I learn about God?
- What did I learn about me?

Find the questions you relate to and ask them to yourself and God. I think God likes questions. It shows Him we are dependent on Him, His teaching, His knowledge, and perspective.

Asking and answering questions is one good Bible study method. There are lots of good Bible reading and study methods. Find one that you are comfortable with. You may even change up over time and explore different methods. I've used many different strategies over the years. You are free to explore whatever is right for you. But pick one and get on with it.

So, quiet time is "daily." That doesn't mean *every day* until Jesus comes. No reason to be legalistic. But a quiet time is a spiritual discipline that should be part of your daily rhythm.

> "No discipline seems pleasant at the time, but painful. Later on, however, it produces a harvest of righteousness and peace for those who have been trained by it." (Hebrews 12:11, NIV84)

Your quiet time needs some structure and personal discipline if you want it to be effective. Here are some foundational parts of a good QT:

1. *Get a Bible you can understand.*

If you have a King James, that's great. I've got one too. But nobody talks like that anymore. Get a NASB or NIV or New Living Translation (NLT). Something you can really read and understand. (I use NASB and NLT together.)

What Bible version do you read? _____

2. *Use a reading plan.*

It will tell you what to read each day and help you stay on track. Pick a simple reading plan that will prescribe a fixed amount for each day. Not too much, but also more than a "verse for the day." *Read the Bible Through* plans are good, but you can get really bogged down at places; they may prescribe more reading than you have time for if you have a job and kids.

3. *Find a place.*

This is important. Find a place where there are no distractions. Your *quiet time* should be in a *quiet place.* A cup of coffee is good. Right now, are you thinking of that place?

Where's your QT place? _____

4. *Find a time.*

You must plan ahead for a morning QT. For most people, morning is the best time. For others, night may be better. Either way, QT will cost you something. And, if we have learned anything so far, God requires us to sacrifice things to Him that are valuable, precious, unblemished. Sacrifice is our way of making God our first priority over possessions and self. *Quiet time will cost you something.* If it does not, then you should re-think it altogether. Give God the first and best of everything. The main thing is to make a "daily" appointment with God, and don't miss it.

What's your QT starting time? _____ AM or PM

5. *Be consistent.*

QT *every day*! Set this as your goal. You won't be able to keep it but try. Think of the words of the Bible as spiritual food. How could you stay healthy if you skip meals or rush your eating? To maintain a high spiritual energy level, you must feed regularly on the Word of God. So, have a daily quiet time.

6. *Don't be discouraged.*

Spiritual growth takes time; it's a crock pot, not a microwave. Be patient, and growth will happen. Do you know someone who is really grounded in the Word, someone you look up to because they seem spiritually mature? Do you know how they got that way? The same way you will. Bit by bit. Day by day. If you miss a quiet time, or a bunch of quiet times (and you will), then just start again. God is always there, waiting on you… to come to Him. He's not keeping score.

7. *Ask for help.*

That person you just thought of who is so grounded? Ask them what they do, what they read, what they find successful, and how they stay consistent.

8. *Write things down.*

Use a journal or diary. You are not reading just to read. Remember, God is speaking here. You would never go into a classroom or your boss's office without something to write on. Your journal can be a fancy leather book with gold edges, or a $1 composition notebook. Or it can be a computer file if that's what suits you best, as it does me. It doesn't matter. Just write things down. When you write something down, you will remember it better, and you can always come back to it for a refresher.

OK, so QT is important; it will cost you something; and it needs a plan. QT includes the Bible and prayer.

But before you do any of that, *worship first*. Worshiping God involves a glorious diversity of options that we can enjoy and employ.

But let's continue to work on *how to worship* in the next chapter.

14

HOW TO WORSHIP

Before NASA will launch a rocket into space, they go through a comprehensive launch status check. The NASA launch director queries all key personnel responsible for the various systems on the space craft and on the ground. He gets a "go/no-go" response from each of the flight controllers. The "big red button" is not pushed until every system is "go for launch."

> *I need to know more about how to worship and to praise my Father, for it's the essential task that connects my temporal life with my eternal one.*
>
> – DAVID JEREMIAH

When every system is perfect, the launch director in Florida will announce, "Houston, we are 'GO' for launch."

"Who may ascend the hill of the LORD? Who may stand in his holy place?
He who has clean hands and a pure heart, who does not lift up his soul to an
idol or swear by what is false." (Psalm 24:3–4, NIV84)

Prior to worship, we must do a system status check as well. Before I can presume to enter into the presence of Holy God, I must check my sin-account status and my attitude status. We have talked extensively about these actions in previous chapters, so I won't go through all that again. But let's summarize it here: since my last QT, has Holy Spirit convicted me of anything displeasing to God? Anything? If so, then a clear and unvarnished confession is in order and a plan for what I am (you are) going to do about it.

- CONFESS & REPENT: "Go for Launch"

Next is a careful attitude check.

- REVERENCE: "Go"
- FEAR/RESPECT: "Go"
- FOCUS: "Go"
- SACRIFICE: "Go, Launch"
- HUMILITY: "Go"
- DELIGHT: "Go, Launch"
- BOLDNESS: "Go"
- CONFIDENCE: "Go"
- HOPE: "Go for Launch"

"Lord, we are **GO** for worship."

"Enter his gates with thanksgiving and his courts with praise; give thanks to him and praise his name." (Psalm 100:4, NIV84)

Just start with this… "THANK You Lord." "I PRAISE You."

Getting started (for me) is the hardest part. Being specific is the next hardest. Just start with "thank you." Then add some specifics.

THANK YHWH for what He has done for you.

- Thank You, Lord.
- Thank You for loving me so much.
- Thank You for saving me even though I disappoint You so often.
- Thank You for helping me yesterday at work.
- Thank You for (your spouse or child, by name).
- Thank You for _____.
- Thank You for _____.

PRAISE Him for who He is to you.

- I praise You, Lord, for being such a good Father to me.
- I praise You, Lord, for showing Your love in so many ways.
- I praise You, Lord, for Your Word. It encourages me so much.

- I praise You, Lord, for _____.
- I praise You, Lord, for _____.

ACKNOWLEDGE His character through His names.

- Lord, You are El Shaddai, my all-powerful, all-sufficient One.
- Lord, You are Yahweh-Yireh, my generous provider.
- Adonai, You are my Shepherd and protector.
- You are my Righteousness and my Sanctifier.
- You are _____.
- You are _____.

Think about your posture. Are you comfortable? Maybe you feel the need to KNEEL, or even lay face down. Your attitude may dictate your posture. You may just want to WAIT on Him to speak. Be SILENT. Clear your mind and listen. (I have to be somewhat physically comfortable to worship. If my knees hurt or the floor is cold, I can't be still or focus.) Do whatever you have to do to shut down and pay attention to His still small voice.

Now, ACKNOWLEDGE Jesus.

- "Jesus, You are my Lord and my Savior."
- "I want to serve You and worship You."
- "Thank You for standing by me and speaking for me to the Father."
- "You are my perfect example to follow."
- "I want to please You and obey You."
- "Jesus, _____.
- "Jesus, _____.

ACKNOWLEDGE Holy Spirit.

- Thank You, Holy Spirit, for teaching me.
- Thank You, Holy Spirit, for being patient with my weaknesses.
- Praise You, Holy Spirit. You are my comforter and helper.
- Holy Spirit, _____.
- Holy Spirit, _____.

Take some of the statements in <u>YHWH in the Psalms</u> in the <u>Appendix</u> and make them personal.

- I **LOVE** You YHWH.
- I **EXALT** You and lift You up.
- I put all my **HOPE** in You.
- I want to **TRUST** You completely.
- YHWH, You are great. You are my shield, my refuge, and my fortress.
- **ABBA**, You are good and ready to forgive. You are merciful and gracious to me.

Be careful here. Don't say things to God you don't really mean! Choose statements and verses that are true and meaningful to you.

You have heard this before, but I want to say it again right here:

> "Yahweh's lovingkindnesses indeed never cease, For His compassions (mercies) never fail. <u>They are new every morning</u>; Great is Your faithfulness." (Lamentations 3:22–23, NASB95 Author's translation added)

If Yahweh's lovingkindness and compassion for us are "new every morning," then perhaps our perspectives on Him could also be new every morning. Every day as we enter into worship, our perspective on God should be fresh. If worship becomes routine or redundant, it is still valid, and God will always welcome our efforts. But for your own joy, as well as for God's pleasure, try to make worship fresh every time you come to Him. The Bible is still your best source for the wonders of Elohim, and the nature and character of Yahweh. Look for creative ideas to bring to worship. Ask others what they do, how they worship. If they don't know what you're talking about, then buy them a copy of this little how-to book.

> "O sing to the LORD a new song, For He has done wonderful things ..." (Psalm 98:1a, NASB95)

OK, all this training in worship may be a lot to remember. Maybe you can keep this book, or your notes close by, just for a reference. You don't have to do all these things every time you worship. Just pick two or three altar **STONES** that you see in these pages and express them from your heart. Say them out loud. If you struggle to get started, then have a go-to song to get your worship launched.

I shared my starter-song earlier.

I love You Lord And I lift my voice
To worship you, O my soul, rejoice.
Take joy my King in what You hear
And may it be a sweet, sweet sound In Your ear.[46]

I just sing this little chorus out loud to Him, right at the start. I sing badly, and my voice cracks in the morning, but Abba is pleased that I made the effort. How do I know that He is pleased? How do *you* feel when you hear your little daughter or nephew or grandson sing in church or at home? Abba loves my singing. And yours.

Worship is how your QT starts, and it doesn't have to last long. You may have limited time for QT. But, when you begin with worship, the Bible will be more alive and real and clear. Your prayer will be richer and more specific and more powerful. How do I know this? I just know. I do.

Some days, you may only want to worship in your QT. That's fine. But this quiet time in the morning is not your *real* worship service. That begins when you light up your second-stage booster and get on with the rest of your day.

> "And so, dear brothers and sisters, I plead with you <u>to give your bodies to God</u> because of all he has done for you. Let them be a living and holy sacrifice—the kind he will find acceptable. <u>This is truly the way to worship him.</u> Don't copy the behavior and customs of this world, but let God transform you into a new person by changing the way you think. Then you will learn to know God's will for you, which is good and pleasing and perfect." (Romans 12:1–2, NLT)

15

RELIGION VERSUS RELATIONSHIP

Re-li-gion/rē li′ jun/ – the belief in and worship of a superhuman controlling power, especially a personal God or gods (*Oxford Languages*).

The primary Greek word that we translate "religion" is used only five times in scripture. It's really more of a secular word. Paul used it once to refer to his former "religion" as a Pharisee and, again, to refer to the worship of angels.

James uses it three times in two verses:

> *God wants worshipers before workers; indeed, the only acceptable workers are those who have learned the lost art of worship.*
>
> – A. W. Tozer

"If anyone thinks himself to be <u>religious</u>, and yet does not bridle his tongue but deceives his own heart, this man's <u>religion</u> is worthless. Pure and undefiled <u>religion</u> in the sight of our God and Father is this: to visit orphans and widows in their distress, and to keep oneself unstained by the world." (James 1:26–27, NASB95)

Here are *my* thoughts on this scripture. James takes his best shot at revealing what makes religion "worthless." He speaks of "pure and undefiled religion," implying that many of those who call themselves "religious" are somehow just the opposite. They cannot control their language, they fail to serve the needy, and they are somehow stained by the sins of the world. In their religion, they are "deceived in their own hearts." When James tries to say something positive about religion, he can only do so with some pretty strong qualifiers. (He reminds me of what his half-brother, Jesus, had to say about the religious elite.)

What *did* Jesus have to say about religion and the religious? If you remember chapter 2, we examined a discussion between Jesus and a Samarian woman about *religion versus relationship*. You may not have understood this at the time, but that's exactly what it was. From there, we dove into the origins of "religion" in the temple worship practices established by God Himself. He put priests in charge of these practices, but priests are human; it wasn't long before they became lazy, selfish, and corrupt. Read the tragic story of the sons of Eli from 1 Samuel 2.

Needless to say, by the time of Christ in the first century AD, things were pretty much out of control. Religious life was corrupt and political, dictated by competing groups of self-proclaimed "scholars" who decided how religious life must work for everyone. The scribes, Pharisees, Sadducees, and the Sanhedrin ruled the religious system. We talked about these guys before. But, just to cut to the chase, let's look again at what Jesus had to say about religious people.

He said the scribes "devoured widows houses..." (Mark 12:38–40, NASB95) He called the Pharisees, "You serpents, you brood of vipers, how will you escape the sentence of hell?" (Matthew 23:33, NASB95) He called the Sadducees "an evil and adulterous generation." (Matthew12:39, NASB95)

The Sanhedrin were the temple priests at the time, and responsible for arresting and trying Jesus. They asked Him if He was indeed the Messiah. His only response to them was "I AM." Then He quoted from the Psalms. They fabricated testimony against Him and condemned Him to death. The Romans performed the crucifixion, but the religious elite killed Jesus.

This wickedness and hypocrisy were the state of religion. But Jesus had come for the explicit purpose of doing away with temple religion and replacing it with something altogether different. When the Pharisees rebuked Him for not following strict religious practices, He said:

> "But I say to you that something greater than the temple is here. But if you
> had known what this means, 'I DESIRE COMPASSION, AND NOT A SACRIFICE,'
> you would not have condemned the innocent." (Matthew 12:6–7, NASB95)

He refers here to the prophet Hosea:

> "For I delight in loyalty rather than sacrifice, and in the knowledge of God
> rather than burnt offerings." (Hosea 6:6, NASB95)

Moving forward from the cross, there would be no need for priests to mediate between the people and God. No need for a temple of stone or an altar with an ever-burning fire.

Jesus would make it possible for everyday people to have a meaningful, personal, everyday relationship with YHWH.

Every individual believer would *become* the temple of Holy Spirit, and every believer would serve as their own priest before the throne of God. Jesus would become our eternal high priest, ever mediating our case before YHWH. His death would become the *final* blood sacrifice to pay for *every* sin – past, present, and future – for *all* who believe. The cross was the final altar and Jesus the final spotless lamb!

> "Do not think that I came to abolish the Law or the Prophets; I did not come to abolish but to fulfill." (Matthew 5:17, NASB95)

"Religion" is not a bad word, really. It's just "one of those words" that has become something it was never meant to be. It has come to represent something we *do* and has lost its original intent altogether. So, I'm going to appropriate the word for my own purposes. I'm going to use it to contrast where many Christians are today with where God *wants* us to be, where we *must* be. In fulfilling the law, Jesus replaced religion with relationship. So, if you consider yourself to be "religious," then try to set that thinking aside. It's completely obsolete.

(Note the check boxes with this list.)
- ☐ Religion is a set of beliefs that include a higher being.
- ☐ Religion is a set of practices designed to earn God's favor (or man's).
- ☐ Religion is a set of check boxes that appease your conscience.
- ☐ Religion is abiding by man-made rules you attribute to God.
- ☐ Religion is doing good because it makes you feel good.
- ☐ Religion is doing good so others will think more highly of you.
- ☐ Religion is rote repetition of religious prayers and words.
- ☐ Religion is just going through the motions because that's what you were taught to do.
- ☐ Religion is trying to be good enough to go to heaven.
- ☐ Religion is writing a check, so you don't actually have to serve.
- ☐ Religion is going to church just so you can say you go to church.
- ☐ Religion is just singing along with the choir. ("This is how I worship.")
- ☐ Religion creates denominations. ("We are right, and they are wrong.")
- ☐ Religion says, "Sure, I believe in God." (But so does the devil.)

Be honest, did you check any of the religion boxes? If that stung a bit, I'm not sorry. But I have some good news for you. There is a cure for religion.

Jesus came to do away with this kind of religion, once and for all. More specifically, He came to "fulfill" the law and the prophets, to complete them by establishing a new way to God, a new way to live in daily relationship with Him. This relationship through Christ is His amazing gift to us, a gift we should gratefully embrace as New Testament Christians.

(Note the check marks with this list. Each one should describe your relationship to God. Add to your list as appropriate.)

- ✓ Relationship is understanding you could never reach God; He had to come to you.
- ✓ Relationship means talking to God on a personal level – one on One.
- ✓ Relationship means realizing what Jesus did for you, then living in a way that honors that realization.
- ✓ Relationship means accepting the constant presence of Holy Spirit in your life and trusting Him to lead you in every aspect of life.
- ✓ Relationship means reading, trusting, and obeying the words of God, written for you.
- ✓ Relationship means loving others in the same way you love, protect, and provide for yourself.
- ✓ Relationship means sharing the love and forgiveness of God with those with whom you come into contact.
- ✓ Relationship means daily worship of the living God, YHWH, our Father and Creator; Jesus, our Savior and Lord; Holy Spirit, our Teacher and Helper.
- ✓ Worship is daily relationship maintenance.
- ✓ Relationship is _____.
- ✓ Relationship is _____.

You and I have been afforded a *personal relationship with the creator of the universe!* Get your hands around that.

For me, when I contemplate the enormity of that gift, my only response is to FALL DOWN and weep and LIFT UP my hands and THANK Him. I want to tell Him how much I LOVE Him. I want to hug Him and BLESS Him and be amazed at His wonderful qualities. I want to SING a song to Him. I sit in SILENCE. I am astounded at what this gift is actually worth to me. To me! I continually want to find ways to demonstrate to God how much He is worth to me. And I want to intentionally put worship first in my life. Through many years of practice, I have learned to make this kind of worship the priority of my life.

It's my heartfelt desire that you can do the same.

16

THE FORTNIGHT CHALLENGE

A fortnight is what the Brits call two weeks. Go figure.

I have a challenge for you.

Every day, for two weeks, I want you to worship God.

(You've come this far, so don't give up on me now that there's homework.)

> *How can you be so dead when you've been so well fed. Jesus rose from the grave and you, you can't even get out of bed.*
>
> – KEITH GREEN

Start on a *Sunday*. My assumption is that you attend church on Sundays. When the worship songs are played, sing *to* God. Address Him directly. Make every segment of the service a worship activity. Worship the Father, and don't do anything else. Stay focused. Review chapters 4 and 5 if needed.

Malachi 3:10 and 2 Corinthians 9:6–8 are your best retirement investment strategies. Remember, I'm retired so I know what I'm talking about. Bring your first, best tenth to the church. Have it ready. Be prepared to give. Your sacrificial giving is an act of worship. See if God will not open up the windows of heaven and pour out an overflow blessing (on you). Refer back to chapter 5.

Set your alarm clock on Sunday night with a quiet time in mind for tomorrow.

Then on *Monday*, have a quiet time before you start your day.

Begin with the right attitudes. Find some stones and build an altar for today. Take a look at the sample altars on the pages that follow. Use these examples or build your own. Keep it simple with just a few stones to start with.

Worship, Bible, prayer. And don't say "Amen."

Now, walk through your Monday with worship on your mind (Ephesians 4:1). Make worship appointments on your smartphone calendar or create reminders with alerts if you need to. Make yellow sticky notes or 3x5 cards with worship scriptures. Make a sticky note for each day with just one altar stone on it. Put it on the dash of your car or on your computer screen. If someone asks you about it, be prepared to "share the hope that is within you" (1 Peter 3:15, NASB95). You have all the tools you need to live your life today with as much worship in it as you can.

At the end of your day, you can close out your "Monday worship service" with an "Amen, Lord. May it be so, every day."

Now, do you see how daily worship works?

Repeat *Tuesday, Wednesday, Thursday, Friday, Saturday.*

Build a daily rhythm. If you can't have a QT one day, just pick it up where you can. Maybe on the way to work or school. It takes time to make new habits and create a worship rhythm. Be patient with yourself.

On the *second Sunday* in the Fortnight, think back on last Sunday and try to improve. Make it different, more sincere, and real. This is *your* service of worship! Add your voice to all the other voices in the room. Be intentional about worshiping in church today, and don't be afraid to let others see and hear you do it. Don't show off but enjoy yourself. If you're not having fun in church, you're not doing it right.

Now make the *second Monday* stronger and more diverse than last week. ACKNOWLEDGE and PROCLAIM God's _____. Cry out to YHWH. Let Him hear you (but don't wake up the baby).

Just SING on *Tuesday.* Maybe dance a little.

Make *Wednesday* a day for READING His Word back to ABBA. ACKNOWLEDGE one of His many qualities. Yahweh, You are _____. (For ideas, look at <u>YHWH in the Psalms</u> in the <u>Appendix</u>.)

Thursday can be solemn with WAITING and LISTENING. REACH your hands out to Him while you KNEEL for one minute in SILENCE. FAST from something today.

On *Friday* REJOICE and be GLAD. DELIGHT yourself in YHWH. Be BOLD.

TEIF! (Thank Elohim It's Friday!)

On *Saturday*, remind yourself of the security you have because Holy Spirit lives inside you. Speak to Him specifically and THANK Him for _____.

Chill out some and think about SERVING others. Have another cup of coffee. Think about doing a little "temple maintenance" today.

OK, now do it again for another fortnight.

And another.

Build this new discipline into your life! Change yourself from an ordinary, well-meaning, churchgoing Christian into an extraordinary, dynamic, daily worshiper. Enjoy God! Bring Him the glory He demands, delights in, and deserves.

One last thought: I trust that you have learned to *worship more and worship better*, and that worship is becoming a priority in your life. Worship is truly a forever pursuit! Every attitude, and act, and acknowledgement you've learned is practice for heaven!

Come, Lord Jesus!

> "And every created thing which is in heaven and on the earth and under the earth and on the sea, and all things in them, I heard saying, 'To Him who sits on the throne, and to the Lamb, be blessing and honor and glory and dominion forever and ever.'" (Revelation 5:13 NASB95)

APPENDIX

Following are several items that you might find useful. This is extra material that you can read or just reference as you need it. Thumb through it or just look at the table of contents below. Be sure to look at the graphics.

Graphics of all the STONES by category. Use these pages as a reference to build a daily worship altar. Then you will find one week's example of altars. Use these or build your own. Always start with the CORNERSTONE.   188

PREPARATION FOR WORSHIP

RIGHTEOUSNESS

PRAY

CLEAN HANDS

PURE HEART

CONFESS & REPENT

BROKEN

CONTRITE

ATTITUDES FOR WORSHIP

BOLDNESS

DELIGHT

REVERENCE

FOCUS

HOPE

FEAR

GLAD

AWE

CONFIDENCE

BROKEN

HUMBLE

CONTRITE

ACTS OF WORSHIP

LOVE

REST

BLESS

BOW

FAST

PRAY

EXALT

TRUST

SACRIFICE

TITHE

CRY OUT

WALK

OFFERING

KNEEL

SERVE

ASCRIBE

SING

REACH OUT

WAIT

SILENCE

READ

PROCLAIM

SUBMIT

MAKE MUSIC

PRAISE

THANK

REJOICE

REMEMBER

ACKNOWLEDGEMENTS IN WORSHIP

LORD

SUFFICIENT   BANNER   REFUGE

SHEPHERD   ASCRIBE   PEACE

ABBA   HEALER   SANCTIFIER   ROCK

SALVATION   PROVIDER   CREATOR

CORNERSTONE FOR WORSHIP

JESUS

SUNDAY WORSHIP

LOVE
SERVE
TITHE
SING
PROCLAIM
PRAISE
REVERENCE
CREATOR
REACH OUT
JESUS
CLEAN HANDS
PURE HEART

MONDAY WORSHIP

LOVE
FEAR
HUMBLE
BOW
WALK
LORD
TRUST
JESUS
BROKEN
CONTRITE

TUESDAY WORSHIP

LOVE
OFFERING
THANK
SERVE
EXALT
LORD
PROCLAIM
AWE
JESUS
BANNER
BLESS
REFUGE
ROCK

WEDNESDAY WORSHIP

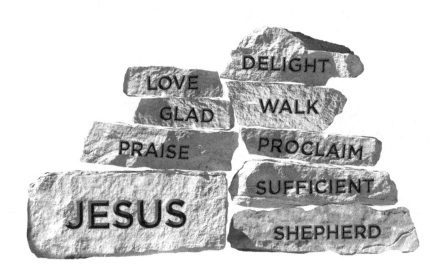

LOVE
DELIGHT
GLAD
WALK
PRAISE
PROCLAIM
JESUS
SUFFICIENT
SHEPHERD

THURSDAY WORSHIP

LOVE
BOLDNESS
BLESS
HOPE
OFFERING
PRAISE
SING
JESUS
REACH OUT
MAKE MUSIC

FRIDAY WORSHIP

HOPE
LOVE
PRAY
FOCUS
THANK
JESUS
CRY OUT
KNEEL
HUMBLE
SACRIFICE

SATURDAY WORSHIP

How I Learn

In the preface of this book, I warned you that I am not a biblical scholar of any sort. But I do study earnestly, and I do manage an original thought every now and then.

I want to understand the words I read in the Bible, in their original language and context. So, I depend on books like *Vine's Complete Expository Dictionary of Old and New Testament Words* (Vines) and *Theological Wordbook of the Old Testament* (TWOT). I have hard copies of these books, but I also have two software tools that I use every day, Wordsearch and Logos. I have an extensive library of Christian study e-books, Vine's and TWOT included, which I access with these programs. I am a computer tech, after all.

I also do research the old-fashioned way: I Google it. I read what others have written on a topic, and I learn from them. I am careful to look for the affiliations and background of the author to discern who's legit and who is not. (Anyone can write anything on the Internet!) I even use Wikipedia, but I try not to let it be the only source on a topic.

I try hard never to plagiarize what others have written. A former preacher of mine once told me, "Preachers never steal another man's crops, but they might glean in their fields occasionally." I do glean, but I suppose we all learn this way. I get bits and pieces from several sources, then make my own explanation of what I learned. I hope this process is fair to my many teachers.

Where I have copied directly or used more than a few lines of a source, I have tried to credit the author in the text and/or in the Citations, Sources and Songs article in the Appendix. Every Bible reference should include its version. I am most fond of NASB95 as I believe it is most true to the original languages.

It is never my intention to use the written or spoken words of others as my own. But I undoubtedly have. If so, I am sorry. I hope you see that my intentions have been honorable, and my words, and yours, are all meant for the glory and worship of our God.

Acts of Worship

This is not a complete list of actions that you may use in worship. These are the acts of worship that I felt needed to be included and explained a bit. I included others, like tithing and sacrifice along the way. Refer to the graphics of the stones starting on page 188 for a more complete view.

Please endeavor to find things that you can do that please God and bring you joy. Have fun!

Names of God

Following is a list of the names included in the book. You might use this list as an overview or to reference a name for worship. This is not an exhaustive list of God's names from scripture; these are just my favorites. I invite you to do your own study into this fascinating topic.[20]

Lord → YHWH → Yahweh → Jehovah

By the 15th century, few Jewish people could read Hebrew because it was no longer their native language. After the destruction of Herod's temple in AD 70, most Jewish people were dispersed over the known world in what was commonly known as the "Diaspora." Soon they only spoke the native language of the lands where they now lived. The ancient Hebrew language was difficult as it was written from right to left and with consonants only (no vowels.) To help the Jewish people read Hebrew, the scribes of the period introduced a system of vowel marks to identify the sounds that were spoken but not written. These marks were placed below, above, or between the consonants of the text. So those no longer fluent in traditional Hebrew could pronounce the words.

When the scribes were confronted with the sacred name of God – YHWH – they were afraid for their readers to say it out loud because it was so holy. God had warned His people never to take His name in vain. Instead of using the original vowel sounds, they placed the vowel points from Adonai – Lord – to indicate that the reader should say "Adonai" instead of YHWH. The vowels a-o-a (adonai) were placed above and below YHWH. Eventually, the first "a" was changed to "e" to prevent the reader from accidentally saying Ya, the first syllable of the sacred name. (Sometimes piety can go way too far!) Christian translators saw YHWH with its e-o-a vowels and changed Ye to the Latin Ja, kept Ho, and WaH became Vah. YHWH became YaHoWeH, which eventually became Jehovah.

This process is called "transliteration," bringing a foreign word into your own language and alphabet. Jehovah is strictly an "anglicized" Hebrew word adapted to English. Many English-speaking Christians have become accustomed to referring to God's covenant name as Jehovah (Jehovah-Jireh for example). There is nothing wrong with using Jehovah instead of Yahweh. Most scholars pronounce God's name as "Yahweh" (Yah-way). (But no one here is claiming too much scholarship.) Over many years, I have moved from Jehovah to Yahweh. I have to admit that it seemed a little awkward and presumptuous at first to refer to God as "Yahweh." But, with practice, reverence, and great care, I'm comfortable with Yahweh and even writing it as YHWH. Modern translations of the Bible still use " Lord " (Adonai) in all capital letters as a replacement name. So, it's just as acceptable to hold the sacred name in reverence and call Him "Lord" (The Lord will provide)." Find out what you are comfortable with, and worship Him by name.

Wave to Jay

Let me tell you the story of Y and its cousin, J.

(It relates to pronouncing and writing the Hebrew names of God we study in this book.)

The English language and many others are based on Latin and Greek. These languages both have alphabets made of discrete letters that, when combined, make-up words. I studied the overly complex story of "Y" online and after just five or six minutes, I was looking for a shortcut, like a e i o u and sometimes y. Sometimes Y is a consonant, and sometimes Y is a vowel. And here's another zinger. Sometimes Y sounds like Yellow, and sometimes Y sounds like Jell-O. Y and J are connected and confusing. And in Spanish, J can be Jell-O, and other times J can be Jose. (¡Estoy muy confundido, Jose!)

So, let's just learn it this way. Y and J are cousins. They are connected, confused, and, at times, interchangeable between languages.

Now, for the story of W and V, also relevant. My friend is Willie in America and "Villie" in Germany. Spelled Willie pronounced "Villie." Any of the Germanic languages will pronounce a W like a V. And the letter V is sometimes pronounced like an F. (Willie ist sehr verwirrt!)

So, it seems that W and V are also connected, confused, and interchangeable relatives.

There are times when we will see Willie and call him Villie, just as there are times when we will see Jell-O and call it Yellow. (I said it was confusing.)

YHWH in the Psalms

The name YHWH appears often in the book of Psalms, which leads and instructs us specifically on how to worship Him. I've listed here a number of these worship statements and declarations from passages in Psalms. I encourage you to use these statements and make them your own in your daily worship. Personalize each one and write it down on this page or in your journal. When you see YHWH, say "Yahweh."

Praise YHWH – "I praise You, YHWH, for your faithfulness."
Worship YHWH – _____
Blessed be YHWH – _____
Give thanks to YHWH – "Thank You, YHWH, for my family."
Magnify YHWH – _____
Sing to YHWH – _____
Sing praises to YHWH – _____
Sing of the lovingkindness of YHWH - _____
Love YHWH – "I love You, Yahweh, because You loved me first."
Fear YHWH – _____
Exalt YHWH – _____
Seek YHWH – _____
Hope in YHWH – "I put all my hope in You."
Trust in YWHW – _____
Boast in YHWH – _____
Rest in YHWH – "I want to rest in Your presence."
Delight in YHWH – _____
Be glad in YHWH – "I am so glad to be with You."
Wait for YHWH – _____
Cry out to YHWH – "YHWH, I need your help!"
Shout joyfully to YHWH – _____
Serve YHWH with gladness – _____
YHWH is great – _____
YHWH is our shield – _____
YHWH is good and ready to forgive – _____
YHWH is merciful and gracious – _____
YHWH my refuge, my fortress – "You are my refuge and my fortress"
YHWH is upright – _____

YHWH is compassionate and gracious – _____

YHWH reigns – _____

YHWH performs righteous deeds – _____

YHWH many are your works – _____

YHWH most high over all the earth – _____

Ascribe to YHWH glory and strength – _____

Ascribe to YHWH the glory of His name – "Your name is above all names."

Holy is YHWH – _____

Gracious is YHWH – _____

Righteous are you YHWH – _____ , _____

Great is YHWH and greatly to be praised – _____

Praise the name of YHWH – _____

Blessed be the name of YHWH – _____

The name of YHWH is to be praised – "Your name is powerful."

The name of YHWH is everlasting – _____

YHWH is my strength and song – _____

YHWH sustains all who fall – "Lord, You lift me up when I fall."

YHWH is righteousness in all his ways – _____

YHWH is near to all who call upon him – _____

YHWH keeps all who love him – _____

YHWH sets the prisoner free – "You set me free from my sin."

YHWH opens the eyes of the blind – _____

YHWH raises up those who are bowed down – _____

YHWH loves the righteous – _____

YHWH protects the strangers – _____

YHWH will reign forever – _____

YHWH supports the afflicted – _____

YHWH favors those who fear him – _____

Citations, Sources and Songs

1   Chapman, Gary. *The 5 Love Languages: The Secret to Love that Lasts* (Northfield Publishing, 2015), http://www.5lovelanguages.com/

2   Pascal, Blaise. *Pascal's Pensees* (Thoughts) Section VII Morality and Doctrine 425 1670, (E.P. Dutton & Co, Inc. 1958), (eBook released 2006 The Project Gutenberg), http://www.gutenberg.org/files/18269/18269-h/18269-h.htm

3   "Worshiper" and "worshipper" are both acceptable spellings for this word. I have chosen to use worshiper because it is the form most common in scriptural texts. Applies also to "worshiped" and "worshiping."

4   Sunshine, Glenn. *Exploring Worship: Part Five, Worship in the Old Testament,* (Breakpoint Colson Center, 2018) http://www.breakpoint.org/exploring-worship-5-worship-in-the-old-testament/

5   Nappa, Mike. *Who Were the Sadducees in the Bible? What Were Their Beliefs?,* (Crosswalk.com Contributing Writer, 2019) http://www.christianity.com/wiki/people/who-were-the-sadducees-in-the-bible-what-were-their-beliefs.html, http://www.MikeNappa.com

6   Wolff, Adrian. Israel - A Chronology Second Edition, (Copyright 2008)

7   Mathis, David. *Worship in Spirit and Truth*, (desiringGod.org – 2014), http://www.desiringgod.org/articles/worship-in-spirit-and-truth#what-it-s-not

8   Boa, Ken. *Who Does God Say That I Am?*, (Bible.org, 2006), http://www.bible.org/article/who-does-god-say-i-am http://www.kenboa.org

9   Parramore, Elizabeth. Spiritual Warfare, http://www.pinterest.com/bpstyler46/spiritual-warfare/

10   Finney, Charles G. *The Memoirs of Charles G. Finney,* 1868 Chapter VI., (as published on Gospel Truth Ministries, Tustin, CA, © 2017), http://www.gospeltruth.net/memoirsrestored/memrest06.htm

11   Cooper, Brad. Sunday sermon entitled, *The Altar of the Heart,* 1/10/21, (courtesy of NewSpring Church, copyright © 2019 NewSpring Church), http://www.newspring.cc/sermons/altars-lighting-the-fires-of-revival/the-altar-of-the-heart

12   Sharpie is a trademark of Sanford, LP and is registered in the United States and other countries.

13   Gay, Ross. *The Book of Delights: Essays*, (Algonquin Books of Chapel Hill, 2019) As heard on NPR's This American Life Podcast

14   *What is fasting and why do Christians do it?* (article courtesy of NewSpring Church copyright © 2019 NewSpring Church) http://www.newspring.cc/articles/spiritual-hunger

15 Lizorkin-Eyzenberg, Eli. *"Hallelujah" in Hebrew Thought*, (Israel Bible Weekly, 2018), http://weekly.israelbiblecenter.com/hebrew-hallelujah/

16 The statement, "The Power of Silence" and the story of Mr. Rogers was used by permission from my friend Jonathan Parker. He teaches churches and businesses the value of Outreach and Conversations from a foundation that is Biblical, Cultural, and Practical. http://www.TheJonathanRParker.com

17 Myrick, Nathan. *History of Hymns: I Love You, Lord.*, (Discipleship Ministries September 2019), http://www.umcdiscipleship.org/articles/history-of-hymns-i-love-you-lord

18 Vander Laan, Ray. *My God is Yahweh*, (That the World May Know, Focus on the Family, 2021), http://www.thattheworldmayknow.com/my-god-is-yahweh

19 Smallwood, Linda. *The God Behind the Names*, (My Redeemer Lives Christian Ministry, 2019), http://www.myredeemerlives.com/namesofgod/yhwh-mkaddesh.html

20 Allow me to suggest two books for further study: Stone, Nathan. *The Names of God*, (Moody Publishers, © 2010) Wilson, Ralph F. *Names and Titles of GOD*, (JesusWalk® Publications Loomis, California © 2010)

21 Stone, Nathan. *The Names of God*, (Moody Publishers, © 2010)

22 Quote: "Music is the language of heaven." Attributed to Ralph Waldo Emerson, Essays, First Series – XI. Intellect. 1841 Also attributed to Mark Lavon "Levon" Helm, American musician, The Band – drummer and vocals. 1940-2012

23 Farran, Kyle. 10 Reasons God Entrusts Us with Trials (ABWE International) Editor's note: Post originally appeared on Kyle's blog on December 8, 2017 and was published on the ABWE Blog February 8, 2019, www.abwe.org/blog/10-reasons-god-entrusts-us-trials

24 Mardis, Roger. *Peaks and Pits* P. 88, (Westbow Press, © 2020)

25 According to *Second Vatican Council, Dogmatic Constitution on the Church Lumen gentium* § 22, 27, the Catholic Pope and Bishops are designated as "Vicar of Christ" with the full authority of Christ over the Church and its members. (Contrast 1 Tim. 2:5)

26 Mote, Edward. *Solid Rock,* (Pastor Rehoboth Baptist Church Horsham, West Sussex, England 1837), http://www.hymnary.org

27 Hall, Mark. Writer, *Who Am I,* Casting Crowns (Beach Street / Reunion / PLG 2004), http://www.musixmatch.com

28 Tomlin, Chris. Songwriter, *Forever,* http://www.christomlin.com

29 Houston, Joel. Hastings, Benjamin William. Tan, Ben. Songwriters, *So Will I,* (© Hillsong Music Publishing 2017)

30 Crosby, Fanny. Songwriter, *To God be the Glory,* 1875, http://www.hymnary.org

31 Cohen, Leonard. Songwriter, *Hallelujah,* (Columbia Records, 1984), http://www.musixmatch.com

32 Luther, Martin. Songwriter, *A Mighty Fortress is our God*, 1529, Hedge, Frederick H. Translator, 1852, http://www.hymnary.org

33 Crosby, Fanny. Songwriter, *Blessed Assurance*, http://www.hymnary.org

34 Klein, Laurie. Songwriter, *I love You, Lord*, (© 1978 House of Mercy Music - admin. Universal Music - Brentwood Benson Publishing), http://www.genius.com/Laurie-klein-i-love-you-lord-lyrics,

35 Croft, Steve. Songwriter, *Pierce My Ear*, Performed by Glad (© 1980 Dayspring Music), http://www.glad-pro.com

36 Newton, John. *Amazing Grace*, (English poet and Anglican Clergyman), 1772, http://www.hymnary.org

37 Carman. Gaither, Gloria. Gaither, Bill. Composers, *His Name is Life*, (© 1983 by Gaither Music Company and Some-O-Dat Music), http://www.musixmatch.com

38 Mieir, Audrey. Songwriter, *His Name is Wonderful,* (Published by: Manna Music, Inc. 1959, 1987), http://www.musixmatch.com

39 Taylor, Steven. Lemmel, Helen. Songwriters, *Turn Your Eyes Upon Jesus*, (© All Essential Music, Nth Degree Songs, New Spring Publishing Inc.) http://www.musixmatch.com

40 Van DeVenter, Judson W. Lyrics, *I Surrender All* (1855-1939) Weeden, Winfield S. Music, (1847-1908), http://www.hymnary.org

41 Newton, John. *Amazing Grace,* (English poet and Anglican Clergyman), 1772, http://www.hymnary.org

42 Mote, Edward. *Solid Rock,* (Pastor Rehoboth Baptist Church Horsham, West Sussex England), 1837, http://www.hymnary.org

43 Fielding, Ben. Morgan, Reuban. *Mighty to Save,* (© 2006 Hillsong Publishing), http://www.musixmatch.com

44 Cline, Thomas. *The Doxology,* 1674, http://www.hymnary.org

45 Lawrence, May F. *Come, O come, let us worship* (Cokesbury Worship Hymnal - © Copyright Lamar & Whitman 1938), Hymn # 295

46 Klein, Laurie. Songwriter, *I love You, Lord*, (© 1978 House of Mercy Music - admin. Universal Music - Brentwood Benson Publishing), http://www.genius.com/Laurie-klein-i-love-you-lord-lyrics

47 Carman. Gaither, Gloria. Gaither, Bill. Composers, *His Name is Life*, (© 1983 by Gaither Music Company and Some-O-Dat Music), http://www.musixmatch.com

48 Johnson, Brian. Davenport, Chris. Songwriters, Come up out of that grave, (© 2019 Bethel Music Publishing (ASCAP) / Shout MP Brio (BMI)), www.musixmatch.com

49 Bullock, Geoff. Songwriter, *King of Kings,* (© So Essential Tunes, Shout! Music Publishing, Hillsong Music Publishing Australia), http://www.musixmatch.com

For the author's blog and additional resources, please visit
the website: http://www.priorityofworship.com

Printed in the United States
by Baker & Taylor Publisher Services